REVOLUTIONARY WAR PATRIOTS *of* JACKSON COUNTY MICHIGAN

Linda Hass and David Van Hoof

THE History PRESS

Published by The History Press
An imprint of Arcadia Publishing
Charleston, SC
www.historypress.com

Front cover: *Washington Rallying the Troops at Monmouth*, painting by Emanuel Leutze (1851) in the public domain. *Back cover, top*: *The Surrender of Lord Cornwallis*, painting by John Trumbull (1819–20) in the public domain.

First published 2025

Manufactured in the United States

ISBN 9781467159562

Library of Congress Control Number: 2025932007

To America's first defenders—in appreciation for the freedoms you fought to give us. And to current generations—may you develop a renewed appreciation for these heroes, for the sacrifices they made and for the benefits we enjoy because of them.

CONTENTS

Forewords, by Rachel Buchanan and Joseph W. Dooley 7
Preface 11
Introduction 15

Part I. Why Jackson, Michigan?
1. What Drew Patriots to Jackson? 21
2. Jackson's First Patriots 24

Part II. Biographies
3. E. Lemuel Benedict 31
4. Sylvanus Blackman/Blackmore, etc. 35
5. Joseph Darling 39
6. Joseph Efner 43
7. John Gibson 46
8. Rhodes (Rhoades) Hall 50
9. David Haynes 54
10. Samuel Hollister 58
11. Daniel Jones 62
12. Abiathar/Abierther Lincoln 65
13. David McGee 69
14. Jabez Mosher Jr. 73
15. Abraham Osborn(e) 76
16. Adam Overacker (Overocker) 80

17. John Perrin(e) 85
18. Isaac Quigley 89
19. Thomas Swartout 94
20. Jonathan (John) Thompson 98
21. Daniel Thurston 101
22. Samuel Underwood 107
23. John Wall 111
24. Swift Woodworth 116
25. Jackson's Mystery Patriots 122

Part III. Jackson's Other Connections to the Revolution
26. A Drum's Journey to Jackson 129
27. A Cannon's Resurrection 132

Appendix A. Request for Help 135
Appendix B. Resources 137
Appendix C. Patriot Cemetery Map 140

Bibliography 143
About the Authors 160

FOREWORDS

In my everyday work with Experience Jackson, Jackson County's official tourism bureau, I find value and connection in my collaborations with Linda Hass. Having known Linda for some time, I can personally vouch for her dedication to the historical preservation of Jackson County and her love of sharing stories that highlight the people involved.

Her work is a labor of love—she doesn't just study history, she brings it to life. I've seen evidence of her immersing herself in archives, walking through cemeteries and traveling the county (and beyond) to gather details that most would overlook. Her unique ability to weave together facts and personal stories is reflected in *Revolutionary War Patriots of Jackson County, Michigan*—a collaborative work with David Van Hoof that gives a voice to the Patriots of Jackson County in a way that few could manage.

Her qualifications, from her master's degree in journalism with a focus on history to her extensive work with state and national designations, only reinforce what her work already reveals—she is a journalist, teacher and historian who is as thorough as she is passionate. She shares this through both her research and writing, along with in-person tours and educational talks locally and throughout the state.

Linda's work also underscores her commitment to bringing people to the crossroads of history, much like this book does. She has not only helped uncover the backstories of these Patriots but has helped ensure that their contributions to our country remain at the forefront of our community's memory. It is my hope, as you read this book, that you will find yourself at a crossroads that connects the past to the present and ultimately to the future of Jackson's—and Michigan's—history.

—Rachel Buchanan
Marketing and Development Manager,
Experience Jackson

I have known David W. Van Hoof for several years. He exemplifies the core values of the U.S. Marine Corps: honor, courage and commitment. Like other Marine Corps officers I have known, he is thoughtful, analytical, rigorous and thorough. These same attributes that served him well in the Marines also shape his approach to researching and writing history.

The Sons of the American Revolution (SAR) encourages its members to write biographies of their Patriot ancestors who supported the cause of American liberty during our War for Independence from Great Britain. Major Van Hoof has written biographies not only of his own Patriot ancestors but other Revolutionary War Patriots as well, totaling twenty-five in all. Each of these is well researched and written in compelling prose.

The SAR also seeks to mark the graves of Revolutionary War Patriots or place historical markers in the cemeteries where these Patriots are buried, such as Woodland Cemetery in Jackson. Major Van Hoof has spearheaded the research into the lives and final resting places of several Patriots and is responsible for placing fifteen historical cemetery markers in Michigan.

Major Van Hoof's passion and expertise for history extend beyond the American Revolution. He has served as an interpretive park ranger at several national parks, including Apostle Islands, Wisconsin; Isle Royale, Michigan; and Katmai, Alaska. He also has served as a park ranger for the Federal Bureau of Land Management at Bear's Ears National Monument in Utah and as a certified interpretive guide/researcher for the National Oceanic Atmosphere Agency in Alpena, Michigan. He has explored the history of lighthouses, shipwrecks and Native Alaskans. He has developed programs, seamlessly weaving history with other disciplines such as archaeology.

Revolutionary War Patriots of Jackson County, Michigan serves as a testament to Major Van Hoof's skill as a historian. The book, in collaboration with Linda Hass, is also a fitting tribute to those Revolutionary War Patriots whose final resting place is in Jackson County and who sacrificed so much for American freedom and the civil rights we enjoy today.

—Joseph W. Dooley
President General (2013–14),
National Society Sons of the American Revolution

PREFACE

Revolutionary War Patriots of Jackson County, Michigan is a collaboration between David Van Hoof and Linda Hass. Van Hoof, a former resident of Jackson County and current resident of Douglas, Michigan, is an attorney and active member of the National Society Sons of the American Revolution. He conceived this project and spent years investigating Revolutionary War Patriots' pension documents; birth, marriage and death certificates; and other sources.

Hass, a Jackson-based author, researcher and trustee of the Jackson County Michigan Historical Society, spent years gathering corroborating evidence, traveling to relevant museums and Revolutionary War landmarks, taking pertinent photos, conferring with various historical experts and writing the book, with help from Van Hoof.

The result is a joint effort that presents a representative sampling of Revolutionary War Patriots who served their country and who either lived in, are buried in or have grave monuments in Jackson County. Each biography gives an overview of the selected Patriot's service rather than a detailed listing of all the regiments under which he served, to keep the biographies reader-friendly for a broad audience. For specific details, please contact coauthor David Van Hoof, who has reviewed hundreds of military documents as part of his research (see the "Resources" section toward the end of the book).

In light of the fact that paper records were rare and infant mortality was high during the Revolutionary War era, the authors have veered away from making definitive statements about how many children Patriots had, choosing instead to focus on the children who moved to or are buried in the Jackson area.

Although findings cannot be verified beyond a shadow of doubt, readers can rest assured that the information presented in this book is based on a preponderance of evidence that includes cemetery documents, military records and pension applications, to name a few sources. Pension applications include the Patriot's sworn affidavits that were reviewed by judges and by federal officials who matched their claims with official musters and roll calls, providing several layers of credibility. Findings also are based on collaborations with state and local historians, museum archivists and cemetery officials and on good old-fashioned legwork in locating and photographing grave monuments.

When presented with conflicting evidence, the authors made deductions based on the majority of reliable evidence. Readers will see, for example, that many biographies include Patriots' birth and death dates and specific burial locations; other biographies do not. This apparent discrepancy is due to a lack of reliable evidence, not oversight.

It is the authors' hope that in fleshing out each biography, these Patriots will be transformed from historical figures described on paper to living, breathing heroes who fought and bled for the country we now call home. This sense of respect is also reflected in our capitalization of the word "Patriot," in compliance with the *Journal of the American Revolution* (JAR) style guide. Retired editorial writer Ken Wyatt also provided editorial guidance.

In a society that increasingly de-emphasizes history, some may claim that a book describing wars fought with muskets and transportation by oxcart is irrelevant. The authors assert, however, that this subject is more than a bygone chapter in the 250-year-old history of our nation. It is a vital topic that is relevant to contemporary readers because it cultivates a shared sense of identity, inspires community engagement and lays the foundation for a legacy that other Americans can build on.

Most importantly for Jackson residents, this book brings a tangible and even personal touch to history through its identification of Patriots' headstones and other relics publicly available within Jackson County. This benefit lends itself to various tours, from schoolchildren to history buffs.

Lastly, the American Revolution itself is relevant to all Americans for many reasons. This pivotal war laid the foundation for our free society. It secured the independence citizens enjoy today. It established our republic form of government dedicated to the interests of everyday people

Grave monuments make history tangible and provide a fascinating backdrop for educational tours such as this one, conducted in Jackson by coauthor Linda Hass. *Courtesy Ed Hass.*

rather than the interests of kings. And it upheld the ideals of liberty, equality, natural and civil rights and responsible citizenship. While the American Revolution did not destroy all inequalities or lead to immediate freedom for all people, it paved the way toward ongoing efforts to live up to those ideals.

INTRODUCTION

The dirty hands that loaded powder and fired muskets during the Revolutionary War (1775–83) have long since ceased their toil. The voices that shouted, "Give me liberty or give me death," no longer ring, and the weary feet that marched up and down the East Coast in all kinds of weather have been laid to rest.

But the democratic system that these Patriots fought and bled for endures to this day. America is no longer a British colony subject to the whims and taxes of a distant king. It is an independent nation that celebrates its 250th anniversary in 2026.

Such a milestone is cause for commemoration, but what of America's original defenders? What of the farmers who set down their plows, the businessmen who abandoned their trades and the youth who risked their lives for the hope of a better, freer tomorrow—does anyone ever pause to celebrate them or consider their trials and tribulations? Why did these Patriots move to Jackson in their sunset years? And why are their stories relevant today? The following pages are intended to answer these questions.

Part I sets the scene by exploring the push/pull factors that motivated America's first veterans to leave the New England states and move to the Michigan Territory. It also suggests why these Patriots chose Jackson in particular and what sights, sounds and experiences likely met them when they first arrived in the fledgling village.

Part II presents the biographies of select veterans, taking a deep dive into their lives. It describes, to the extent possible, their upbringings, their motivations for serving in the War for Independence, their marriages and

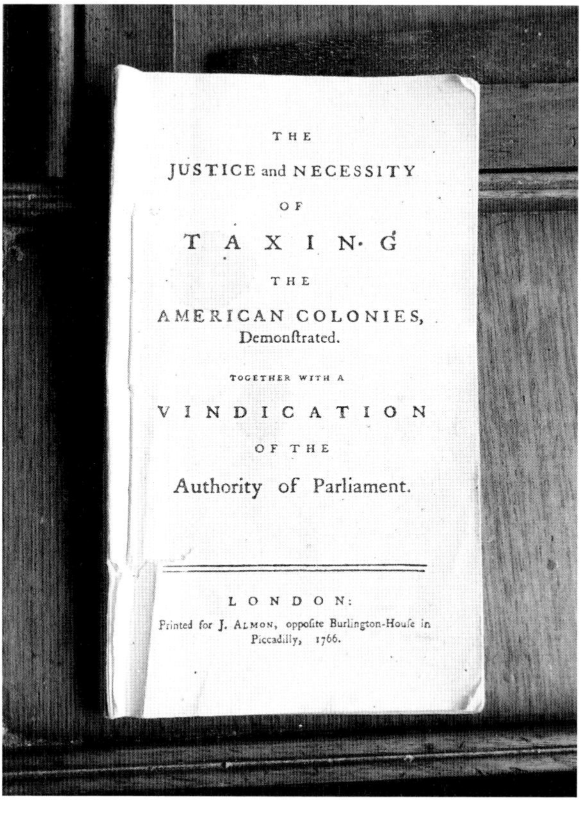

THE

JUSTICE and NECESSITY

OF

TAXING

THE

AMERICAN COLONIES,
Demonſtrated.

TOGETHER WITH A

VINDICATION

OF THE

Authority of Parliament.

LONDON:

Printed for J. Almon, oppoſite Burlington-Houſe in Piccadilly, 1766.

Above: This 1876 lithograph by Currier & Ives depicts Patrick Henry's "Give me liberty or give me death" speech before the Virginia legislature in 1775. *Wikimedia Commons.*

Left: This book, published in London in 1766, defended the British position of imposing taxes on American colonists. *Photo by Linda Hass, courtesy #thisismackinac.*

THE AMERICAN REVOLUTION IN A NUTSHELL

Prior to the American Revolution, the Original Thirteen Colonies were governed by Great Britain, one of the greatest military powers of that time. When the British government levied taxes without the input or representation of American colonists, the resulting political disagreements triggered a cycle of defiant acts on the part of colonists and correspondingly punitive laws on the part of Great Britain. It's worth noting, however, that taxes were just one dispute among many that sparked a revolutionary spirit. This growing discontent led to open rebellion and, ultimately, war between the British army and American Patriot forces, organized as the Continental army and commanded by George Washington. The Patriot forces, with the assistance of France and Spain, defeated the British, achieved independence and ultimately formed the United States of America.

families and their sunset years, including where they were buried. It also explores several mystery Patriots whose evidence seems persuasive at first glance but is questionable upon further examination.

Part III examines Jackson's other connections to the American Revolution, including a 1,407-pound relic that was manufactured in England and made various journeys on—and under—water and was used in the American Revolution. This piece of field artillery made a final trip to a local museum that now has the distinction of displaying one of the oldest such pieces in Michigan's military history!

The appendices present opportunities for follow-up, including a resource guide showing various organizations, museums and sites in Michigan that present information about the Revolutionary War; a map of Jackson County showing where Patriots are buried; and contact information for those who have additional information about Patriots buried in Jackson County.

The authors hope that their treatment of this subject will enable readers to walk a mile in the boots of America's original defenders, develop a personal connection with these Patriots and cultivate the kind of tangible connection that a visit to a cemetery can provide. Ultimately, this book is designed to bring these Patriots back to life, if only in readers' hearts and minds. As you read the stories of those who sacrificed so much for Americans' liberty and freedom, prepare to be moved, enlightened and sometimes surprised.

PART I

WHY JACKSON, MICHIGAN?

Chapter 1

WHAT DREW PATRIOTS TO JACKSON?

What drew Revolutionary War Patriots who were born and raised in the New England states to the hinterlands of the Great Lakes—and to the humble burg of Jackson in particular? By the time Jacksonburg became an official village in 1830, these Patriots would have been in their seventies and eighties—not an ideal age to venture into a roughhewn village that demanded much of its hearty pioneers.

In fact, it's interesting to consider whether the thought of moving west was even a twinkle in Patriots' eyes during the Revolutionary War (1775–83). The Proclamation of 1763 established by the British discouraged colonists from moving west of the Appalachians due to the dangers of living in an unprotected wilderness—not exactly an inducement to travel! And when the Northwest Territory that included Michigan and four other Great Lakes states was established in 1787, the prospect of moving to an undeveloped area was still a risky bet, although trappers and other explorers had been doing so for years.

In spite of these deterrents, at least twenty-two Revolutionary War Patriots chose to either move to Jackson in their sunset years or live close enough to be buried in this county. Why? And what were their experiences once here? No evidence has been found to date shedding light on their exact reasons for moving to Jackson, but their travel from the New England states in the early to mid-1800s mirrors a general migration westward, prompted by many push/pull factors.

Numbers That Tell a Story

Numbers tell a story when it comes to the Patriots who moved to Jackson County. When analyzing their origins, destinations and ages, a picture emerges of very sturdy stock from the New England states—trailblazers who were willing to take risks on an unproven settlement in the thick of the woods. The majority of these men hailed from Massachusetts (six), with Connecticut and New York claiming the second-largest number of veterans (five each). The earliest settler arrived in what is now Jackson County in 1831—only one year after the village was settled—and the latest in 1851. Most settled in Sandstone Township (four), with Napoleon and Columbia townships as close seconds (three each). The majority of Patriots were in their seventies and eighties when they arrived; many lived into their nineties—and one died at ninety-seven!

Among pull factors, acreage in the Northwest Territory became affordable to the average person when the cash-strapped government searched for ways to fund governmental services and pay off debts incurred by the Revolution. The fastest and easiest way to generate money was to sell land at bargain rates, with some prices as low as one dollar per acre. Many adult children of Patriots took advantage of this perk and moved to the Michigan Territory, as it was known before statehood, seeking a new, affordable start on land of their own.

In addition, experts contend that soil in the New England states is generally rocky. This push factor inspired many pioneers to migrate to Michigan and the Ohio Valley, which had soil much easier to till. Several aging veterans, eager to spend their sunset years with their descendants, followed in their children's footsteps.

Even Patriots whose children did not move to Michigan were drawn to the territory because of bounty land warrants authorized by the Revolutionary War Congress for military service under the acts of 1788, 1803 and 1806. A bounty land warrant was basically a grant of free land issued to veterans in return for military service from the Revolutionary War through 1855. These warrants allowed eligible veterans to claim land in the public domain.

Additionally, the 1825 completion of the Erie Canal, which runs east–west between the Hudson River and Lake Erie, became the first navigable waterway connecting the Atlantic Ocean to the Great Lakes. This new liquid thoroughfare reduced the costs of transportation and accelerated settlement of the Great Lakes region.

The resulting westward migration and influx of European-descended people had disastrous ramifications for Native Americans already inhabiting the land they had considered home for thousands of years—a topic deserving attention in and of itself. Nevertheless, cheap land was a powerful inducement for small farmers with big dreams and an incentive for the many Patriots who ultimately migrated to Michigan.

Chapter 2

JACKSON'S FIRST PATRIOTS

One of the earliest Patriot homesteaders to arrive in Jackson was Joseph Darling, a Massachusetts native of Scotch descent who traveled to Michigan with his family and possessions via boat through the Erie Canal. Once in Detroit, the resilient Patriot purchased oxen and a wagon and continued the long journey through "the almost impassable wilderness" to the fledgling village of Jacksonburg.

Arriving from the east, he would have entered the village via St. Joseph Street, which today is known as Michigan Avenue. Likely, he arrived in the warm months, when he would have seen Indian cornfields in the distance and immense forests that covered much of the county in a lush canopy of green. This would have reassured him that the burg had fertile soil and abundant lumber—important resources for any homesteader. In addition, streams crisscrossing the area would have gurgled the presence of clean, drinkable water—another reassurance.

Upon the Darlings' entry into town, they would have passed a small collection of log buildings erected by "brave, hearty pioneers" in a "sparsely settled" county. Settlers weren't the only presence in the community, however. Wolves were so plentiful that in 1833, the county board of supervisors offered a $2.50 bounty for the scalp of any full-grown wolf killed within three miles of the dwelling of any inhabitant. Obviously, pioneer life was not for the faint of heart!

Thomas McGee, son of Revolutionary War Patriot David McGee, wrote about his family's trek to "Oak Openings," a clearing about one and a half

Many Revolutionary War veterans who moved to Jackson County would have lived in rough-hewn log cabins similar to this one. *Photo by Linda Hass, courtesy Ella Sharp Museum, Jackson, Michigan.*

miles north of what today is the Village of Concord. His father, a Patriot from Massachusetts, would have been about seventy-two years old when the McGees made this journey. Upon arrival at their property, family members got to work building a communal log cabin and roofing the structure with shingles cut by hand. They also built a chimney of mud and fieldstone collected from their property.

An especially popular destination for incoming Revolutionary War Patriots was Sandstone Township, propelled to fame by one of the most thriving villages in southern Michigan at the time—the Village of Barry. If it had endured, the village would have been located near the intersection of West Michigan Avenue and Sandstone Road. When Patriots Abiathar Lincoln of Massachusetts, John Perrin(e) of New Jersey and John Wall of New York moved to Sandstone Township in the early 1800s, Barry rivaled Jacksonburg in commerce, prestige and potential. The village's undoing began around 1839, when its bank collapsed. This led to its eventual demise. Fortunately, the township had other draws that prompted residents to remain in that fertile spot, albeit elsewhere within Sandstone's boundaries.

Another hotspot for Patriots was Columbia Township, with its new sawmill and scenic lakes. David Haynes of Pennsylvania and Jabez Mosher and Thomas Swartout, both of New York, moved near the Village of Brooklyn between 1837 and 1839 so they could be near their respective families. They also likely appreciated the township's many assets. One local historian described "Clark's Lake" in the heart of the township as "one of the most beautiful sheets of water in southern Michigan."

Clean water, fertile soil and abundant game were among local resources that benefited all residents. In addition, living near or with family in Jackson County provided an advantage before support systems such as social security existed. Jackson also offered these aging Patriots one more thing—a final resting place. In fact, it was the presence of their grave monuments that inspired this book.

But Patriots didn't just reap benefits from moving to Jackson County; they also left their mark on the rich tapestry of the county's history through their many contributions. David McGee passed on a fierce love of freedom that inspired his descendants to participate in the secret system known as the Underground Railroad. The McGees were among agents who opened their homestead to freedom seekers and transported them by wagon from Concord to the next stop along the west–east corridor. The daughter and son-in-law of Patriot Adam Overacker, a New York native who moved to Grass Lake in 1833, also opened their home to freedom seekers who spent the night there and then traveled on to Detroit, a major launching point into Canada.

Joseph Darling brought with him a valuable contributor to the fledgling community—his wife, Huldah Darling. The couple arrived in Jackson around 1832, and she apparently provided residents with the rare benefit of a female knowledgeable about healing. Some sources refer to Huldah as "doctor." While no evidence has been found to date shedding light on her specific training, it was not unusual for women to have specialized knowledge of healing and midwifery. Huldah's skills undoubtedly were helpful to pioneers at a time when doctors were scarce.

American Revolutionary War Patriots also left their mark on Jackson County through their very presence. They were a physical reminder of the ongoing liberties that all Americans benefit from—liberties that were very costly to defend in blood and treasure. In this sense, these Patriots represented a worn, blood-red thread interwoven in the tapestry of Jackson County's ongoing history—a brilliant but brief strand that ended when the last Patriot was laid to rest. And while these original defenders may be gone, they are not entirely forgotten, thanks to their headstones, other monuments and lineage-based organizations dedicated to honoring these first veterans.

Contemporaneous documentation shows that early residents held these old Patriots in high regard and even felt a sense of awe about them. The obituary in honor of Patriot John Thompson, who moved from New York to Michigan around 1833, is a good example. The memorial, in the May 25, 1847 *Jackson Citizen*, bemoaned: "How few of the fathers of the revolution remain! We trust he has gone to his eternal rest, where wars are known no more."

Hopefully, today's generations will be inspired to have the same awe and respect for these freedom fighters who left their homes, livelihoods and families to stare death in the face for the prospect of establishing the liberties that future generations could enjoy and build on. The legacy they left for Americans is truly monumental. Find out more about them, including their trials, tribulations and triumphs, in the following chapters.

PART II

BIOGRAPHIES

Chapter 3

E. LEMUEL BENEDICT

Born to: Jonathan and Elizabeth Benedict in 1764
Birthplace: Warren, Connecticut
Moved to: Jackson County in or before 1839, in his seventies
Died: October 11, 1839
Burial: Spring Arbor Cemetery, Spring Arbor Township

For many Patriots, taking up arms against Great Britain was a matter of principle and pragmatism. Principle, because the British Parliament had levied taxes on colonists without giving them any say in that government's policies, resulting in rebellious acts that spurred even more punitive measures. But the Revolutionary War was also a matter of pragmatism because colonists wanting to supplement their incomes could be hired as substitutes for those who did not serve in the war for various reasons. As surprising as this practice may seem to modern readers, hiring paid substitutes was a tradition that extended to the Civil War but ended with World War I (see "The American Revolution and the Draft").

E. Lemuel Benedict, a Patriot from Connecticut, was such a substitute, serving in place of his father, Jonathan Benedict. An article in the June 5, 1924 *Jackson Citizen Patriot* describing memorial services held by the National Society Daughters of the American Revolution (NSDAR) shed light on the reason for Lemuel's substitution. It stated: "At the age of 15, he [Lemuel] served three months in place of his father, who was temporarily disabled." If accurate, it would mean Lemuel began service as a fifteen-year-old in 1779.

This is the grave monument of E. Lemuel Benedict, who is buried in Spring Arbor Cemetery, Spring Arbor Township. *Courtesy Linda Hass.*

Sixteen was the youngest official age for service during the Revolutionary War, and Lemuel would have met that threshold in 1780, given his birth year of 1764. Nevertheless, many authorities looked the other way when capable fifteen-year-olds like Lemuel volunteered to serve, especially when manpower was low.

Documentation on the exact nature of Lemuel's service as a substitute has not been found yet, but given his father's varied assignments throughout the Revolution, Lemuel would have had several opportunities for action. The elder Benedict was listed on the rolls of the Connecticut militia with Captain Daniel Hickock's company for several engagements and served for one year as an orderly sergeant in the regular army at West Point.

Wherever Lemuel served and whatever battles he participated in, he must also have waged a private war in his mind, wondering if his father would recover from a disabling injury and if their sacrifices on behalf of a new nation would lead to victory or defeat. While the outcome of his father's injury is unknown, the successful outcome of their sacrifices is the reason for our nation's 250th anniversary!

Five years after the war ended, twenty-four-year-old Lemuel married Annis Hickox/Hitchcock (1769–1814) in Danbury, Connecticut. The couple had several children. Life was hard in the early 1800s, and Annis was among those who died young by today's standards—at the age of forty-five. She is buried in Connecticut. Presumably, Lemuel's father is also buried in one of the New England states. After Annis's death, Lemuel and his children began a westward migration across New York until 1832, when he and son Moses Benedict moved to Michigan. They were followed by other family members, including Lemuel's sisters, Mary (Benedict) Morris and Abigail Hannah (Benedict) Riggs, and their spouses and children.

Sometime in or before 1839, Lemuel moved to Jackson County. His interests and occupations when he settled in Jackson County are unknown, but if his son's community involvements are any indication, Lemuel likely instilled a strong sense of civic duty in his children. Moses Benedict (1796–1865) is mentioned on several pages of DeLand's *History of Jackson County, Michigan*, beginning with Moses's move in 1832 to the "infant colony" in what is now Concord Township. In subsequent years, Moses was listed as running for sheriff and belonging to a Masonic Lodge in Concord Township. Presumably, his father lived nearby or in neighboring Spring Arbor Township.

On October 11, 1839, at the age of seventy-five, the former teenager who dutifully served as a substitute for his injured father during the American Revolution ended his last assignment on earth. E. Lemuel Benedict was

The American Revolution and the Draft

American Revolutionary military forces drafted men throughout the war (1775–83). The draft process generally worked like this: state militias divided their contingent into classes of fifteen to twenty men and then called out (drafted) one or several of a county's classes for service that ranged from weeks to months. After men served the allotted time, they returned to their homes. Hired substitutes were allowed to serve in place of men drafted for various reasons, including a willing volunteer who wanted the pay and hardship caused if a bread earner was compelled to leave his farm or business to serve.

buried in Spring Arbor Cemetery. The 1924 newspaper article previously mentioned stated that the initial "E" before his name stood for the first name of his mother, Elizabeth. Likely, it remained an initial only. Lemuel's son and daughter-in-law Moses and Elizabeth (Welch) Benedict were buried in the same cemetery nearby.

Lemuel was not the only underage Patriot who served as a substitute during the Revolutionary War and moved to Jackson in his sunset years. The next story tells the tale of another young freedom fighter who followed a similar path.

Chapter 4

SYLVANUS BLACKMAN/BLACKMORE, ETC.

Born to: James and Sarah Blackman/Blackmore on April 28, 1764
Birthplace: Gloucester, Providence County, Rhode Island
Moved to: Napoleon Township in or before 1837, in his seventies
Died: Before 1854
Burial: Unknown, likely Napoleon Township

Like E. Lemuel Benedict, Sylvanus Blackman, a Patriot from Rhode Island, also was a paid substitute—not once but four times for different men, beginning with a short stint in 1777. Service that year for someone born in 1764 would have meant that Sylvanus was very young for military service. Regardless of his exact age, this early teen was willing to take on adult responsibilities at a critical point in our country's history and face all the dangers inherent in that choice.

Sylvanus's other times of substitution were in June 1778 for one month, later in the summer of 1778 for fifteen days and in July 1779 for one month, with all substitutions occurring in Rhode Island. No evidence has been found to date of his personal experiences during the war, but the youngster must have known there was no guarantee he would return home unscathed—or at all—since at least twenty-five thousand colonists died in the Revolutionary War, according to historians.

The loss of a son to grieving parents is incalculable. But such a loss in an agricultural-dominated society also had practical implications. It could mean one less helping hand in planting and harvesting crops, one less person to tend to livestock, one less bread earner and, as a result, less food for a hungry family.

This sketch of a minuteman from the American Revolutionary War was created by Brianne Witt, Spring Arbor University associate professor of art. *Courtesy Linda Hass.*

Fortunately, Sylvanus survived the war, returning home to contribute to his family. He married sometime later. Not much is known about his wife other than her name—Mehitable. It's also unknown how many children the couple had, but documents show they had at least one son. The family lived in Worthington, Massachusetts, for many years and then moved to Onondaga County, New York, where they remained until 1804. The estate documents for his father—James Blackman—show that Sylvanus inherited his father's apparel and five dollars, suggesting that the family was not prosperous. Sometime in 1804, when Sylvanus was in his forties, the couple moved to the "howling wilderness" of the Michigan Territory, and by 1806, they rented a farm northwest of Detroit.

In civilian life, the Patriot showed the same industriousness as in the war, serving as marshal of Detroit's Huron District in 1811 and as clerk of the Woodward Avenue Market in 1819. Originally, Woodward Avenue was a Native American trail called the Saginaw Trail, which stretched all the way to Saginaw, Michigan. The trail was later converted into a wood planked road to assist in carriage and wagon travel; hence the derivation of the name—Woodward Avenue. It wasn't long before this well-traveled area became a market hub.

Sometime in or before 1837, the couple moved to Napoleon Township. In 1837—the same year Michigan became a state—seventy-three-year-old Sylvanus filed for his service pension with the Circuit Court of Jackson County. Although the Circuit Court judge found his service worthy, Sylvanus's application was denied because he had not served the requisite six months (see "Revolutionary War Pensions"). According to the 1840 U.S. census, seventy-six-year-old Sylvanus was still a resident of Napoleon Township at that time.

Sometime before 1854, the Patriot who willingly defended his homeland and survived the Revolutionary War succumbed to Father Time. The location of Sylvanus's grave is yet to be determined, but since he lived in Napoleon during his last days and there is no record of him moving anywhere else afterward, he is likely buried in that township. In 1854, Sylvanus's son, Wilson of Edwardsburg, Cass County, Michigan, was listed as the executor of his father's estate.

Given the deviations of the Blackman surname, Sylvanus's other relatives may have been Nathaniel Blackmar of Jefferson Township, Michigan, and Charles Blackmar of Cambridge Junction, Michigan. It is also interesting to speculate whether Sylvanus Blackman was related to Jackson's founder, Horace Blackman (1801–1850). There is no proof of that to date, but both

Revolutionary War Pensions

On August 24, 1780, the Continental Congress passed the first act offering pensions to widows and orphans of Revolutionary War soldiers. In 1818, Congress passed another law granting pensions to Revolutionary War veterans based on financial need. Congress amended the law several times, with the most liberal pension legislation enacted in 1832. This act gave full pay for life to officers and enlisted men who had served for two or more years and partial pay for service of six months to two years. In fact, some Patriots gave up their 1818 pension and reapplied for the 1832 pension because it was more generous.

historical figures were born in the New England states and both moved to Jackson County.

The next chapter tells the tale of another teen who was not only ready to fight at a minute's notice but was willing to maneuver one of the most ingenious blockades used in the Revolutionary War.

Chapter 5

JOSEPH DARLING

Born to: Benjamin and Hannah (Harris) Darling on September 22, 1764
Birthplace: Middleborough, Massachusetts
Moved to: Jackson County circa 1833 in his late sixties
Died: circa 1844
Burial: Woodland Cemetery, Summit Township

Imagine volunteering to serve in a fledgling militia against one of the most experienced fighting forces in the world, and—adding to the odds stacked against you—now also imagine you are only fifteen years old. Those challenges are among many that make the life of Joseph Darling interesting.

Joseph and his family were colonists from Massachusetts who supported independence from Great Britain. He enlisted with the militia in his home state on June 1780, serving as a private. Joseph was among many technically underage youths to enlist, being three months shy of his sixteenth birthday.

The Revolutionary War has often been compared to the proverbial battle of David and Goliath, except in this case, the red-coated Goliath was one of the greatest economic and imperial powers of the world at that time, while American militias were often ragtag groups of dedicated civilians. Did that inequity give Joseph cause for concern? If so, he did not let it deter his determination to fight for independence.

Joseph's first company was tasked with repelling British troops in Newport, Rhode Island. Soon after being discharged from duty, he volunteered as a minuteman—that is, a civilian ready to fight at a minute's notice. In September, he was called to rendezvous with other militiamen

THE GREAT CHAIN

From the beginning of the American Revolutionary War, the Hudson River was considered an essential inlet. To halt British ships from progressing to vulnerable communities along the river, in 1778, Patriots forged an iron chain that stretched across a narrow bend near the river's entrance. The seventy-five-ton chain, which rested on a log boom, was a successful deterrent. It was removed each winter of the war to avoid destruction by ice and reinstalled each spring. One can only imagine how difficult it must have been for soldiers like Joseph Darling to pull it out! Several iron links remain on public display today at the United States Military Academy at West Point in New York.

at Wrentham, Massachusetts, where they formed into a Massachusetts Militia company. The company then marched over two hundred miles to West Point, New York, where it relieved Continental army forces so they could support General George Washington's siege at Yorktown, Virginia.

The siege was effective. On October 19, 1781, British General Lord Charles Cornwallis, one of the leading British officers, surrendered. Although Joseph did not directly participate in the siege, his militia was among reinforcements that helped to make it possible—an initiative that ultimately paved the way for a major turning point in the Revolutionary War.

One fascinating milestone that Joseph did participate in, however, was pulling out the "Great Chain" that stretched across the Hudson River. In December 1781, Joseph's company was tasked with extracting the seventy-five-ton iron chain that served as a barrier preventing British ships from sailing up the river and accessing inland New York (see "The Great Chain"). One can only imagine the physical strain endured by soldiers in pulling the heavy, ice-cold chain ashore in the winter and then going back to their tents or drafty military barracks to sleep. Likely, Joseph's young age was among factors that helped him endure the extreme elements. After the chain was successfully extracted from the harbor, Joseph's company was discharged from service. His accumulative service of six months qualified him for a pension.

In 1787, Joseph married Huldah Cotton (1766–1841). The couple had several children, at least three of whom are buried in Jackson County. The

GREAT CHAIN AND MORTARS.

Above: This sketch illustrates links of the Great Chain at West Point, New York. It was designed to deter British ships from sailing up the Hudson River. *Wikimedia Commons*.

Left: This is the grave monument of Patriot Joseph Darling and his wife, Huldah Darling, who are buried in Woodland Cemetery, Jackson. *Courtesy Linda Hass*.

Darling family, of Scottish descent, lived in several New England states before moving to the Michigan Territory via the Erie Canal around 1833. Once in Detroit, sixty-nine-year-old Joseph purchased oxen and a wagon and traveled with his family through "the almost impassable wilderness" to the fledgling Village of Jacksonburg, which was at that time "a mere collection of a few log buildings." The tract of land he purchased at $1.25

per acre included portions of what is now considered the City of Jackson.

On November 12, 1833, Joseph filed for his pension to be forwarded to the Jackson County Court, signing his name with an *X*. His pension was approved several months later, and he received twenty dollars per year from the government. Another fascinating facet of Joseph's personal life is that his wife, Huldah, is credited as being one of Jackson's first female doctors. Details of her professional life have not yet been discovered, but her knowledge of healthy living may explain why she exceeded the average lifespan of about forty years at that time.

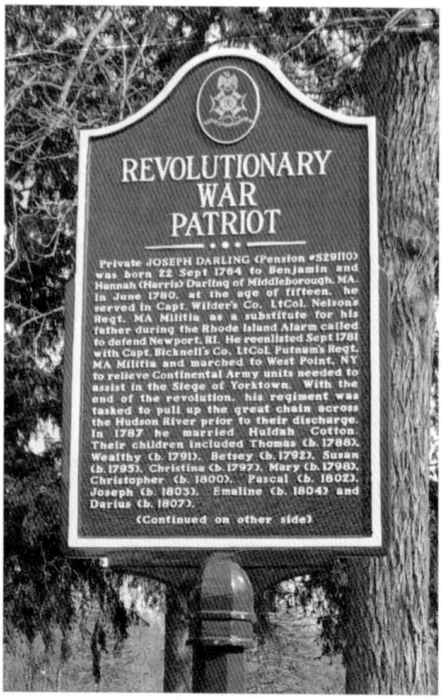

This historical marker, near the grave of Patriot Joseph Darling, gives fascinating details about his life. *Courtesy Linda Hass.*

Huldah died on October 5, 1841, at the age of seventy-five. Joseph, who "spent his last years with his children," died on June 3, likely in 1844, around the age of eighty. Their three children buried in Jackson are Dorinda (Darling) Laverty (1802–1833, buried in Leoni Cemetery), Josephus Darling (1803–1867, buried in Maxon Cemetery) and Eveline (Darling) Laverty (1806–1892, buried in Woodland Cemetery).

The tale of Joseph and Huldah's interments also follows an intriguing path. The couple was initially buried at the old East Main Street Cemetery, which was Jackson's original burial ground directly to the east of today's Henry Ford Hospital on Michigan Avenue. The cemetery was not well maintained, and over time, it became an eyesore. The property itself, however, was considered a prime spot for Jackson's expansion, so the graves were relocated and the property was made available for development. In the process, the Darlings' graves were moved to Woodland Cemetery on Francis Street.

Joseph's grave monument was rededicated in 1918 by the Algonquin and Sarah Treat Prudden chapters National Society Daughters of the American Revolution. On November 12, 2023, Joseph's grave was further distinguished by the installation of a historical marker sponsored by the National Society Sons of the American Revolution in cooperation with the City of Jackson. This marker was researched by coauthor David Van Hoof.

The next chapter describes the ordeals of another teenager who served in the Revolution and marched hundreds of miles to help desperate colonists.

Chapter 6

JOSEPH EFNER

Born to: Valentine and Catrina Efner on November 1, 1759
Birthplace: New York, New York
Moved to: Leoni Township in 1842 at eighty-three years
Died: July 8, 1843
Burial: Unknown, likely in Leoni Township

While many Patriots served at least six months during the American Revolution, Joseph Efner went above and beyond, serving from one to several months for almost every year of the Revolutionary War. Joseph enlisted with the Albany County, New York Militia in September 1776. The first of many tours for this seventeen-year-old began with a fifty-mile march to Fort Edwards, New York, to reinforce Patriot forces there.

In August 1777, he fought in two conflicts in New York: the Battle of Freeman's Farm, also known as the First Battle of Saratoga (September 17, 1777), and the Battle of Bemis Heights (October 7, 1777). The former battle, which was the bloody culmination of months of posturing, occurred shortly after Joseph arrived, immersing the teen in a baptism of fire, with hundreds of soldiers killed, wounded or captured on both sides. The latter battle was also hard fought but resulted in a major American victory that became one of the turning points in the Revolutionary War.

After the second battle, Joseph's regiment marched to the smoldering town of Esopus, New York (today known as "Kingston"), arriving two days after the town was burned to the ground by British forces (see "Revolutionary

Building, staffing and protecting forts like this one were important duties for many American Revolutionary War soldiers. *Photo by Linda Hass, courtesy #thisismackinac.*

Flames"). His unit, which probably helped desperate colonists regroup and rebuild shelters, was discharged shortly thereafter, likely with blazing scenes of war seared in his memories.

The seasoned Patriot had many more tours in which his unit was called upon to reinforce forts, guard farmers, support Patriot troops and escort British prisoners back to Albany, New York. In October 1780, his regiment was attacked by British forces and their Iroquois allies. It could have responded in many ways, from retreat to holding its ground. What the confident regiment chose to do, however, was counterattack, which it did with such gusto that its enemies were repelled and chased for twenty miles until its former attackers were successfully dispersed. Joseph's last tour of service was in November 1782, when his regiment provided security at Middle Fort, now in Middleburgh, New York.

Four years after the war, Joseph married Ruth Doty (1759–1798) in New York. The couple lived in various places throughout the state and had several children, at least one of whom is buried in Jackson County. Life in the 1700s was tough, and lifespans were often short, but Ruth's life was especially short. She died on March 25, 1798, at the tender age of thirty-nine and is likely buried in New York. There is no record of Joseph

Revolutionary Flames

The town of Kingston, Ulster County, New York, has had various names in its past, from Esopus to Wiltwyck to Kingston, the name used today. During the American Revolution, this scenic town on the banks of the Hudson River was torched by British forces—an act that has been described by historians as one of the "most heinous" for that area during the American Revolution. This act of desperation was part of the British army's campaign to wrest control of the strategically vital Hudson River from Patriot forces. The wanton burning, during the month of October 1777, had the opposite effect, however, adding fuel to colonists' revolutionary furor and quickening the determination of men like Joseph Efner to fight for freedom.

remarrying. Records show that in 1833, the seventy-four-year-old widower filed for a pension, which was approved.

In October 1842, at the age of eighty-three, the Patriot moved to Leoni Township to live near his daughter. On July 8, 1843, four days after a Fourth of July celebration that soldiers like Joseph helped to make possible, the warrior who had willingly served when asked breathed his last. Joseph's grave has been lost to time, but he was likely buried in Leoni Township, where he last resided. His grave is probably near the grave of his daughter, Catharine (Efner) Young (1795–1855, buried in Maxon Cemetery, Leoni Township). While Joseph's grave site has not yet been located, this does not diminish the respect this Patriot deserves for giving his all to his new country at a time when it needed him most.

Most of the biographies in this book focus on the exploits of individuals such as Joseph. In reality, however, these individuals were part of units that formed strong bonds of shared experiences as soldiers who served together for the common goal of forging an independent nation. The next chapter illustrates the depth of fellowship that many Patriots shared.

Chapter 7

JOHN GIBSON

Born to: James and Martha (Campbell) Gibson on August 3, 1752
Birthplace: Voluntown, Connecticut
Moved to: the Village of Jackson ("Jacksonopolis")
around 1838, in his mid-eighties
Died: July 3, 1848
Burial: Unknown, likely Mount Evergreen Cemetery, City of Jackson

John Gibson's story is a testament to the fellowship of comrades-in-arms, not only during active military service but in civilian life as well. John, of Connecticut, enlisted as a private with the Regiment Rhode Island Line in January 1776 when he was twenty-four years old. Serving with him were William Richardson and Amos Perkins, both of Rhode Island. This threesome shared many wartime experiences, including firing on British warships and constructing an earthwork battery near what today is Fort Adams State Park, Newport, Rhode Island.

These earthworks usually took the form of a ditch and a protective earthen wall or mound around the rim. They offered considerable protection when bullets were flying but could be a muddy mess in the rainy season. In May 1776, the regiment was folded into Continental forces, and in September of that year, General George Washington sent the regiment to eastern Long Island to reinforce troops there.

The paths of the threesome parted in October 1776, when William Richardson left to become a marine and Amos Perkins left to become an orderly sergeant for another company. John stayed with the company as a private and went on to participate in a deadly amphibious operation that ultimately captured twenty-three (British) Loyalist soldiers at Brookhaven, New York. John survived this brush with death, but it was costly: six British Loyalists and one Patriot were killed, and several soldiers were wounded on both sides.

In November, John's company was sent to Newport, Rhode Island, to bolster militia forces there. However, when Newport was invaded by a large force of British and Hessian (German) troops in December 1776, the outnumbered Patriot forces withdrew. John's enlistment period ended in January 1777, when he was discharged.

After returning home, John married Ruth Anthony Brown (born January 22, 1763). The couple had several children and resided in Voluntown, Connecticut, as late as 1785. In 1820, while residing in Norwich, New York, the sixty-eight-year-old Patriot sought a pension for his military service. In his application, he described himself as a butcher with limited use of his left hand due to rheumatism. According to his application, he had no real property, and his personal possessions consisted of a horse and wagon, two hogs, two axes, a cleaver and three knives for a total value of $38.25. In light of the above and considering that his occupation required manual dexterity that he didn't fully possess, it's likely he was experiencing hard financial times.

Pension approval was not a given. The federal government denied applications for various reasons, including the applications of some Patriots described in this book. But the three comrades who stood side by side in war reunited for mutual support in their pensions as well—each providing

Jackson's Name Changes

In 1829, New York native Horace Blackman registered a claim for 160 acres in what is now Jackson at two dollars per acre. In 1830, Blackman's claim was named "Jacksonburg" in honor of then-president Andrew Jackson. A few years later, postal officials changed the name to "Jacksonopolis" to avoid confusion with other Jackonburgs. Townspeople later shortened the name to the one used today, "Jackson." In 1841, the Village of Jackson was incorporated, and in 1857, Jackson became a city.

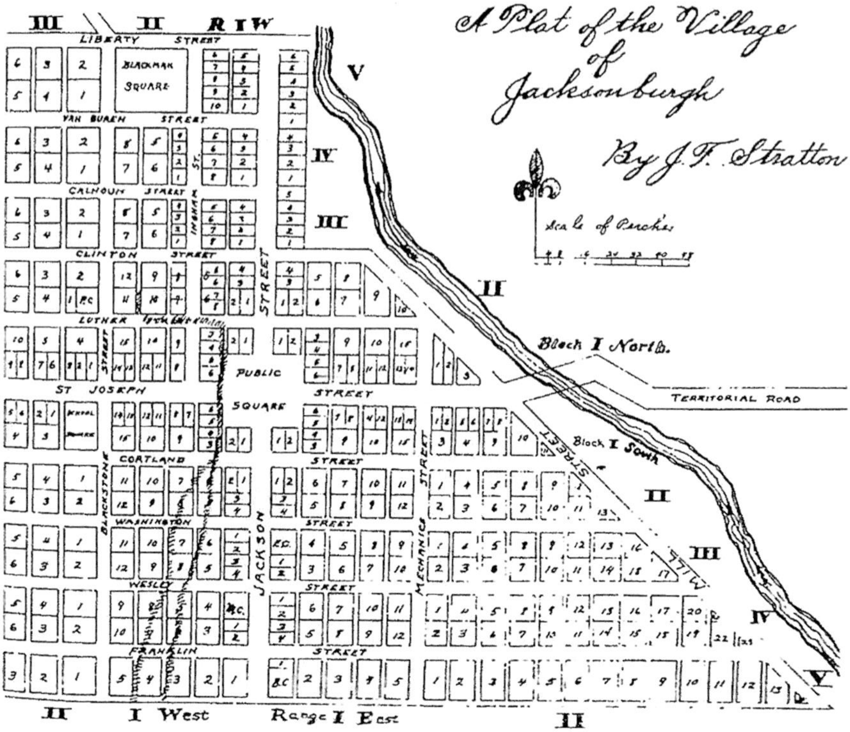

Patriot John Gibson likely would have been familiar with the various names of his new home, from "Jacksonburgh" to "Jacksonopolis" to "Jackson." *Courtesy Jackson District Library.*

statements that validated the other's service. The show of force was effective—John's pension was approved in March 1821, as were the pension requests of William Richardson and Amos Perkins.

Around 1838, at the age of eighty-six, John moved from New York to Jackson to be near his children. Originally called Jacksonburg, the town's name was later changed to Jacksonopolis and then finally shortened to its current Jackson (see "Jackson's Name Changes"). On October 27 of that year, he requested that his pension be transferred to Jackson. The indefatigable Patriot lived for another ten years; then, one day short of the Fourth of July celebration that John and other Patriots fought to make possible for our country, the soldier whose worn and aching hands cut and packaged meat and built earthworks returned to the earth. John Gibson died on July 3, 1848, at the incredible age of ninety-six.

No burial monument has yet been discovered for this Patriot, but he is included in this book because there is no record of him living anywhere but Jackson in his last days. It is unlikely a ninety-six-year-old would have moved to a different county at that late stage in his life—especially when his children continued to live in Jackson County. Also, there was no subsequent pension transferal request after Jackson.

In addition, son Amasa bought a plot in Jackson's Mount Evergreen Cemetery (block 5, range 2, lot 4) for his wife, Mary Hay Douglass Gibson, who died in 1852. Amasa was also buried in the same cemetery in 1868, suggesting this was a family plot and hinting that John was also buried there in an unmarked grave. Regardless, the absence of a headstone does not diminish the respect owed to this Patriot who put his life on the line to help America gain its independence.

The Patriot described in the next chapter also faced challenges when it came to getting his pension application approved. While he didn't call on his brothers-in-arms for backup, he did call on his blood brother for reinforcement.

Chapter 8

RHODES (RHOADES) HALL

Born to: Theodoty and Elizabeth (Hall) Rhodes on March 23, 1757
Birthplace: Westerly, Rhode Island
Moved to: Grass Lake Township around 1836 at seventy-nine years
Died: September 21, 1840
Burial: Unknown, likely in Grass Lake Township

Rhodes Hall endured a barrage of assaults during the American Revolution, from cannon bombardments to the burning of a town. But it was a different kind of fire that most threatened this beleaguered veteran many years after the war.

Rhodes, a Patriot from Rhode Island, enlisted in the Continental army in 1776 at the age of nineteen. During his multiple tours, he constructed fortifications, participated in several battles and engaged in covert missions such as the plan to attack British fortifications in the seaport town of Newport, Rhode Island. To launch the surprise attack, his militia accessed a whaleboat, but as the boat approached Newport, the British unleashed withering cannon fire.

What would it have been like to crew that boat and watch whizzing cannonballs burst on you from the depths of darkness, only to sail past your head and plunge into the sea, unleashing a flurry of waves that rocked the boat? One can only wonder what feelings and fears this teen experienced on this tumultuous night. Outgunned, the whaleboat retreated, and the mission was abandoned—but the war effort continued.

Rhodes Hall fought with soldiers from the First Rhode Island Regiment, represented by the soldier on the left in this illustration. *Wikimedia Commons.*

In August 1778, Rhodes's militia joined forces with the Continental army and French troops in a combined effort to once again wrest Newport from British control. The conflict culminated with the Battle of Rhode Island (or Battle of Quaker Hill) in August 1778, an unsuccessful effort in which 30 Patriots were killed and 173 were wounded. Of special interest is the fact that among those participating in this joint effort was the First Rhode Island Regiment. This regiment, often called the "Black Regiment," was composed of African-descended Patriots (see "Black Patriots").

Rhodes's service also is linked to another famous—or, in this case, infamous—chapter of the Revolutionary War. In 1781, Rhodes's unit was called to render assistance to the smoldering town of New London in nearby Connecticut, following its blazing destruction. Upon orders of traitor General Benedict Arnold on September 6, 1781, New London was looted and torched by British soldiers and Loyalists (see "Traitor Benedict Arnold Orders Town Burned").

No documentation has been found on the type of assistance Rhodes's unit rendered, but it likely included protecting inhabitants from further attacks and helping to build shelters for homeless residents. The destruction of civilians' (as opposed to combatants') homes and places of work was another grim reminder of devastation unleashed by Arnold, a former resident of Connecticut and America's most infamous traitor.

Black Patriots

Rhodes Hall, a Revolutionary War Patriot who moved to Jackson County around 1836, was among Patriots who fought alongside 5,000 African-descended people on the Patriot side in the American Revolution. A Continental army roster among Washington's papers lists 755 "black" soldiers in fifteen different brigades of Washington's main force at White Plains, New York, in the summer of 1778 alone. Blacks also served in the Eleventh Continental Regiment from Rhode Island. Later in the war, the regiment was transformed into the First Rhode Island Regiment and became what is considered the first all-Black regiment in American history. At the end of the Revolution, General George Washington stated that Black and white soldiers together endured "almost every possible suffering and discouragement" with a level of perseverance that "was little short of a standing miracle."

After the war, Rhodes married a woman whose name cannot be conclusively determined at this time. The couple, who had at least one son, lived in various towns in Rhode Island and New York. As a result of his moves, at some point after his discharge, Rhodes inadvertently burned his discharge papers. It was this fire that caused him considerable grief because veterans' pensions required discharge papers for proof of service. Most Patriots made great sacrifices during the war, including disrupting their occupations. They also sustained life-altering injuries, including amputations. As a result, many Patriots were unable to work after the war and became impoverished.

Such was the case for Rhodes, who applied for assistance under the Congressional Act of 1818 to provide for veterans in reduced circumstances. To compensate for the lack of discharge papers, his brother Adam filed testimony on Rhodes's behalf. Apparently, the request was not approved, because in June 1833, Rhodes filed once again for a pension. Fortunately, his second application was approved in November of that year, granting the seventy-six-year-old $42.44 per year.

Documentation shows that Rhodes moved to Grass Lake Township around March 1836 to reside with his son, whose name and burial location have not yet been verified. Although Rhodes's wife's name is unknown, documentation proves he was married since he is identified as a "widower" when he moved to Jackson County.

Traitor Benedict Arnold Orders Town Burned

Major General Benedict Arnold's performance at the Battles of Saratoga (New York, September/October 1777) contributed to the American victory there, but a bitter rivalry with Arnold's commander led the turncoat to treason. As a British brigadier general, Arnold ordered his command to burn the town of New London, Connecticut, including buildings owned by noncombatants. This cruel act sealed Arnold's reputation as an infamous public enemy. His name has since become synonymous with "traitor." Interestingly, a monument to Arnold was erected in Saratoga National Historical Park, New York, in 1887, in recognition of his service at the Battle of Saratoga. Because Arnold severely injured his leg in the battle, the monument depicts his boot and explains the battle but does not mention him by name!

On September 21, 1840, the eighty-three-year-old Patriot who had survived so many assaults in defense of his country breathed his last. His exact burial location is a mystery, but it is likely the Grass Lake area, since that is where he lived during his last days and there is no record of him moving anywhere else after Grass Lake. While his exact grave site is unknown, his record of service lives on.

Rhodes wasn't the only Patriot to face bureaucratic challenges due to paperwork snafus. The veteran summarized in the next chapter was actually apprehended and detained when he could not produce the proper paperwork. Read on to find out more about his interesting story.

Chapter 9

DAVID HAYNES

Born to: Bartholamew and Jane Haynes on April 13, 1762
Birthplace: Paxton, Pennsylvania
Moved to: Columbia Township in 1837 at seventy-five years
Died: April 2, 1844
Burial: Jefferson Cemetery, Columbia Township

If you had served faithfully in the military yet were charged with desertion due to a paperwork snafu, would you reenlist with that same military? David Haynes faced that exact situation, and his response might surprise you.

David was a Patriot living in Northumberland, Pennsylvania, shortly before the war. Not much is known about his mother, but his father, Bartholamew Haynes, owned forested land and wanted David and his brother, James, to be proficient marksmen. So Bartholamew bought his young sons muskets, and over the years, the boys' marksmanship lived up to their father's expectations. They also became very familiar with the twists and turns of various paths through the dense woods.

This knowledge of the terrain came in handy in 1777, when the family's home was converted into a garrison stronghold to protect residents from raids conducted by British forces, Loyalists and their Iroquois allies. Fifteen-year-old David served as an unofficial scout during this time, guiding Patriot patrol detachments through the path's twisting networks.

David and his brother officially enlisted in the local militia in 1778, when David was sixteen. They served multiple tours, usually several months at a time. They also acted as rangers and spies scouting along a twenty-five-mile-long path. All went well until the fall of 1779, when, after being discharged from a tour, the brothers returned home. Much to their surprise, they were apprehended as deserters because they could not find their official discharge papers.

The dismayed teens surrendered their equipment, including their guns, to authorities (see "Revolutionary War Equipment"), and while James was held as "collateral," David was released to obtain the needed documentation. One can identify with the panicked feeling of misplacing something vital—perhaps a credit card or a cellphone—and the frantic search to retrieve it. But in this case, the solution was not as easy as retracing one's steps, since the lads had traveled up and down a twenty-five-mile-long path. Questions likely raced through David's mind—Would he be able to get his brother out of confinement? Would they both get their treasured muskets back?

Unable to retrieve the lost papers, the industrious teen obtained alternate certification from a Patriot colonel. Then he raced back to James's captors with the needed documentation in hand. It did the trick, and much to their relief, both brothers were free to go—along with their guns.

Remarkably, that was not the end of David's service. Undaunted by the false charge of desertion, the nineteen-year-old reenlisted in October 1781 as a substitute. After one month of marching to various locations, the unit was discharged and all returned home, including David—this time, with his discharge papers in hand.

After the war, David married Margaret Ewart (1775–1836) on March 30, 1790. The couple had several children, at least one of whom is buried near

Revolutionary War Equipment

When properly supplied, the typical soldier in the Continental army carried about forty-five pounds of gear that included his musket and bayonet, a cartridge box, a powder horn (usually a cow or ox horn), a haversack (small cloth bag worn over the shoulder), a knapsack (like a backpack), a tin cup, a canteen, a bowl, a spoon and, if lucky, an extra blanket and shirt. The militia soldier generally carried weapons from home, such as axes and muskets, as well as homemade accessories. The illustration on the back cover provides a good illustration of the various equipment used.

Top: Smoothbore muskets like this "Brown Bess" were among the most commonly used weapons in the American Revolutionary War. *Photo by Linda Hass, courtesy #thisismackinac.*

Bottom: This is the grave monument of Patriot David Haynes, who is buried in Jefferson Cemetery, Columbia Township. *Courtesy Linda Hass.*

Jackson County. After living in various New England states, the seventy-one-year-old Patriot applied for his pension in 1833. It was approved.

Sometime after Margaret's death in 1836, the widower moved to Michigan to be near his son Jonathon Haynes (1802–1864, buried in Somerset Cemetery, Hillsdale County). On October 16, 1837, David, then seventy-five, requested that his pension be transferred to the post office address in Brooklyn, Columbia Township. The village had been founded five years prior by Calvin Swain, who filed the first land claim on June 16, 1832, and originally named his settlement Swainsville. Likely, residents were still calling it by that name when David arrived, since the name "Brooklyn" was a fairly recent phenomenon, established in 1836 in honor of Brooklyn, New York.

On April 2, 1844, almost seven years after David arrived, the eighty-one-year-old Patriot died just a few days short of his eighty-second birthday. The former marksman is buried in Jefferson Cemetery, Columbia Township, on a hill overlooking Lake Columbia. The high vantage point with views in all directions might have pleased the former trail scout.

Like David, many Patriots enjoyed strong family ties with their parents and siblings. The Patriot described in the next chapter not only came from a long line of revolutionaries, but he also went out of his way to retrieve his recuperating brother and bring him home. Read on to find out more about this fascinating story.

Chapter 10

SAMUEL HOLLISTER

Born to: Joseph and Rachel Hollister on March 24, 1764
Birthplace: Sharon, Connecticut
Moved to: Sandstone Township in the 1830s in his mid-sixties
Died: 1842
Burial: Chapel Cemetery, Sandstone Township

Patriot Samuel Hollister was born into a family of revolutionary activists, beginning with his father, Josiah Hollister, who served in the Albany County, New York Militia. Samuel's three brothers also served in several militias, and two of his brothers signed the 1774 boycott of British goods—a radical act that preceded the American Revolutionary War.

The torch of freedom burned brightly for the Hollister family, whose members lived in several New England states over the years. Little wonder that Samuel followed in his family's footsteps at seventeen, enlisting with the Third New York Regiment in 1781. The regiment was tasked with supporting General George Washington's Continental forces in Albany, New York. Their duties included guarding northern forts along the Hudson River (Fort Ann, Fort Edward and Fort George) and blockading British forces in New York City.

The blockade was necessary because not only had British forces taken control of Albany, but they had also begun using the city as the center for British political and military operations. This, in turn, led to an influx of British Loyalists from other colonies into the city and an exodus of Patriots out

Many Revolutionary War forts, like the one guarded by Patriot Samuel Hollister, were located along rivers. *Photo by Linda Hass, courtesy #thisismackinac.*

of the city. However, by November 1783, the blockade and other measures had so crippled the British bastion that British forces finally vacated, paving the way for the triumphant return of General George Washington and his Continental forces.

A personal episode for Samuel during the war revealed the close ties that the Hollister family experienced. During one mobilization, Smith Hollister, one of Samuel's brothers who also served in a militia, remained in the Albany military hospital three weeks beyond the expiration of his term. Samuel was sent to retrieve his brother, only to be told by the physician that Smith would not survive the bumpy wagon ride home. So, Samuel patiently waited until the physician finally cleared Smith—a wait amounting to five weeks—before bringing him home to their anxious family.

As a point of comparison, how long would today's sibling be willing to wait at the hospital to take a brother or sister home? A few hours? A few days?

And what did Samuel do during the five weeks he waited? The answers to these questions are unknown, but it is known that Samuel showed incredible patience on behalf of his brother.

Four years after the war ended, Samuel married Betsey/Betsy Smith (1766–1855) of Ballston, New York. The couple, who lived in New York and Connecticut, had several children, one of whom is buried in Jackson County. In the 1830s, Samuel, Betsey and their son Henry moved to Jackson County, settling in Sandstone Township.

It is interesting to speculate on the possible connection between this move and the promotion of Sandstone Township by a former New York resident, Samuel Roberts. In the early 1830s, Roberts bought 160 acres in the township near the intersection of Sandstone Road and West Michigan Avenue. Then he filed a plat for a village he named "Barry" and aggressively marketed the attractive, fertile land to fellow New Yorkers, offering lots from $25 to $100.

Whether or not the Hollisters were motivated by Roberts's marketing, they were among several Patriots who moved to Sandstone Township. Ironically, the village of Barry gradually faded into obscurity as an administrative entity, but the township itself continued to grow, counting among its residents the Hollisters.

In 1842, the Patriot whose militia helped expel the British from New York City during the war and who went the extra mile to fetch his sick brother died at the age of seventy-eight. Samuel Hollister was laid to rest in Chapel Cemetery, Sandstone Township, near his son Henry Hollister (1800–1861)

Medical Care During the Revolution

Doctors' medical knowledge during the Revolutionary War was very basic and often flawed, according to "The American Revolution: An Everyday Life Perspective," an online offering from New York University. Doctors and nurses during this time were scarce, and many lacked formal training. Hospitals were rare, medical instruments were rudimentary and the causes and treatments of common ailments remained a mystery. Soldiers also had to contend with the close quarters, poor sanitation and hygiene and contaminated food and water supplies—all of which contributed to the rampant spread of disease in army barracks.

This is the grave monument of Patriot Samuel Hollister, who is buried in Chapel Cemetery, Sandstone Township. *Courtesy Linda Hass.*

and daughter-in-law Harriet Hollister (?–1877). Samuel's widow, Betsey, is buried in Milwaukee, Wisconsin, near other family members who had moved there. On November 12, 2023, a Revolutionary soldier plaque was placed on Samuel's grave by the Louisa St. Clair Chapter, National Society Daughters of the American Revolution.

The military exploits of Patriots who moved to Jackson are well represented in this book, but there was another aspect of service that had little to do with exploits or battles. Read on to find out more about this less dramatic but ever-present challenge.

Chapter 11

DANIEL JONES

Born to: Isaac and Thankful Jones on July 1, 1756
Birthplace: Dighton, Massachusetts
Moved to: Grass Lake Township before 1847, between eighty and ninety years
Died: April 14, 1847
Burial: Unknown grave, Oak Grove Cemetery, Napoleon Township

Massachusetts native Daniel Jones did not fight in any major Revolutionary War battles nor have any near escapes from enemy clutches, but the Patriot's service with the Massachusetts Militia likely reflected everyday hardships that deserve mention. Daniel was a private in the Bristol County, Massachusetts Militia, serving in various tours throughout his home state as well as Connecticut and Rhode Island from 1776 to 1780. His units' missions included responding to alarms when British forces threatened portions of this territory, confronting enemy troops and providing support for coordinated efforts to repel the British.

These are the duties that officially defined his service, but there is another under-reported aspect that marked his and almost every other Patriot's service—the struggle to find adequate food. At one point during the war, as starvation and desertion rates began to increase for Patriot forces, a desperate General George Washington wrote that his army must "inevitably be reduced to one or other of these things: Starve, dissolve, or disperse."

It is interesting to note how paltry rations were for these active men (see "Revolutionary War Diet"). Historians note that many soldiers would go on independent hunting expeditions to supplement their meager rations, and

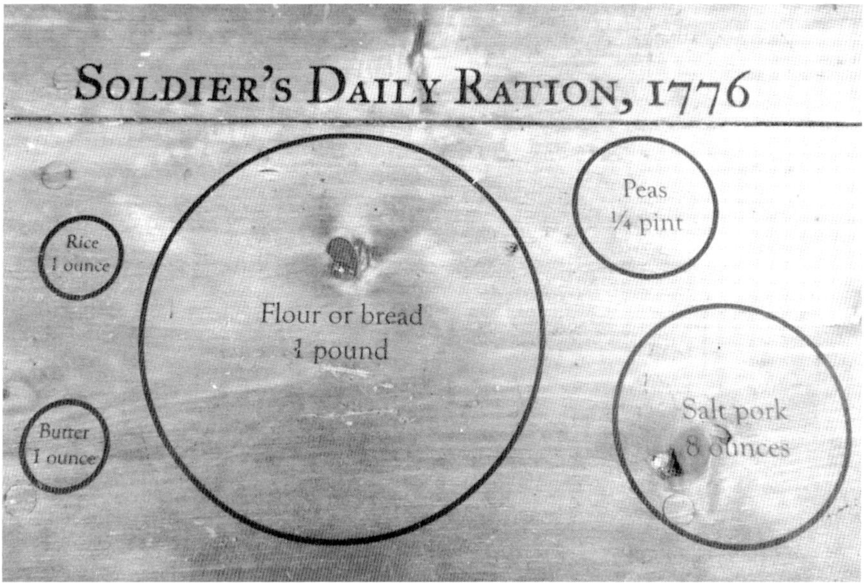

This diagram illustrates a soldier's daily ration in 1776, with bread composing the majority of the diet. *Photo by Linda Hass, courtesy #thisismackinac.*

some desperate soldiers even raided area farms. Was Daniel among those who went on scavenging excursions for such commonly sought-after plants as berries, morel mushrooms, watercress (an aquatic plant in the cabbage family) and sorrel (a leafy green vegetable)? Did he slip away from his post to hunt game? It is unknown, but it is known that Daniel was among the survivors of the war and its corresponding hardships.

In 1781, three months before the British surrender at Yorktown, Virginia, Daniel married Bethany Pierce (1761–1847) of Dighton, Massachusetts. The couple had several children. Sometime before 1847, Daniel and Bethany moved to Grass Lake Township, Jackson County, to be near or live with their son Joshua Jones (1787–1868, buried in Oak Grove Cemetery, Napoleon Township). Their daughter Thankful Jones (1792–1868) is also buried in Oak Grove Cemetery.

Details of Daniel's and Bethany's life together in the fledgling village have not been found to date, but DeLand's *History of Jackson* offers some insights into the pioneering days of the Jones family in Jackson County, suggesting that the Jones men were quite strong. DeLand states, "There was a number of Jones families among the pioneers of Jackson County.…These muscular and strong-willed men have all been laid away in their last sleep."

REVOLUTIONARY WAR DIET

It is not known exactly what Patriot Daniel Jones ate during his service with the Massachusetts Militia, but on June 10, 1775, the Massachusetts Provincial Council set the following daily rations for its troops in Boston:

- 1 pound of bread
- ½ pound of beef and pork; except one day in seven—1¼ pounds of salt fish
- 1 pint of milk
- 1 quart of spruce or malt beer
- ½ cup peas or beans

Not all soldiers actually received these rations, but this list was the council's best recommendation for an entire day. The council also set an allowance of one pound of soap for six men per week. Other colonies set different ration quantities, as they were able. In spite of minor differences, bread remained the main staple.

On April 14, 1847, the Patriot whose weary feet marched through three states in defense of his country was laid to rest at the age of ninety-one. Records show that Daniel was buried in Oak Grove Cemetery, Napoleon Township, although his exact burial site is unknown. Bethany died that same year at the age of eighty-six and also is buried in an unknown grave in Oak Grove Cemetery, Napoleon Township. Likely, their burial sites are near their son and daughter, Joshua and Thankful Jones, in the same cemetery.

Like the Patriots who foraged for food, the freedom fighter described in the next chapter made himself at home in the forests, taking advantage of every nook and cranny in the great outdoors. But his goal was not scavenging for sustenance—it was conducting the kind of unconventional warfare that contributed to an American victory. His tactics would not be surprising to twenty-first-century readers, but in Revolutionary War times they were, well…revolutionary.

Chapter 12

ABIATHAR/ABIERTHER LINCOLN

Born to: Daniel and Hannah (Leonard) Lincoln on June 4, 1759
Birthplace: Taunton, Massachusetts
Moved to: Sandstone Township in 1837 at seventy-eight years
Died: October 22, 1844
Burial: Chapel Cemetery, Sandstone Township

Abiathar Lincoln's record of service during the Revolutionary War is a tribute to the guerrilla warfare that helped to weaken one of the greatest military forces at the time. Abiathar, a Taunton, Massachusetts Patriot, enlisted in the Massachusetts Militia in June 1776 at the age of seventeen. During his many tours of service that stretched into the fall of 1777, the units he served with built fortifications, enforced blockades against the British and reinforced the Continental army in Massachusetts and Rhode Island, among other duties.

Abiathar's units also participated in various raids as well as hit-and-run tactics that continually harassed the enemy. Records of Abiathar's personal experiences in this type of guerrilla warfare have not been found, but it is a matter of record that this tactic wore down British forces and ultimately contributed to Patriot successes (see "The Importance of Guerrilla Warfare in the Revolution").

One can almost envision the teen hiding behind boulders and ridges in the shade of a dense forest, questioning the wisdom of long lines of British Redcoats marching under the hot sun in clear, open sight. Specialized British

Left: This is the grave monument of Patriot Abiathar Lincoln, who is buried in Chapel Cemetery, Sandstone Township. *Courtesy Linda Hass.*

Below: The top of Patriot Abiathar Lincoln's headstone is distinguished by the engraving of his given name. *Courtesy Linda Hass.*

> **THE IMPORTANCE OF GUERRILLA WARFARE IN THE REVOLUTION**
>
> During the American Revolution, the Continental army was significantly outnumbered by the British army. As a result, many Patriot forces resorted to unconventional forms of warfare that included hit-and-run attacks, ambushes and sabotage. This type of warfare had several advantages: it capitalized on inhabitants' knowledge of the terrain, including good spots for ambushes; and it was affordable, since no special uniforms or equipment were required. It's worth noting that General George Washington opted for conventional grand battles with the British most of the time, but he also recognized the value of unconventional warfare, which was an effective deterrent that helped to weaken the resources of the British army and drive up the cost of the war for Great Britain.

troops, including mounted infantry called "dragoons," were known for their speed and maneuverability, but it was more typical for long lines of men, three ranks deep, to march in unison, since this formation was thought to be able to unleash the most destructive firepower at one time.

After the war, Abiathar married Mary Babbitt (1767–1837) in Norton, Massachusetts, on August 24, 1783. The couple, who resided at various places in New Hampshire and Vermont, had several children. On April 3, 1833, while living in Bennington, Vermont, the seventy-three-year-old Patriot filed for a pension, which was granted.

As the aging veteran considered where he wanted to spend his sunset years, he and Mary decided to move to Sandstone Township sometime before the fall of 1837. The couple's son and daughter had already moved to Jackson County and are buried there. Anna (Lincoln) Wood (1792–1857) is buried in Chapel Cemetery, Sandstone Township, and Abiathar Lincoln Jr. (1786–1853) is buried in Fifield Cemetery, Blackman Township.

But the couple's time together in their new home was short. On November 18, 1837—the same year that Michigan became a state—Mary died. She is buried in Chapel Cemetery, Sandstone Township. Abiathar lived with his daughter and son-in-law, Anna and Jothan Wood, for seven more years. On October 22, 1844, at the age of eighty-five, the Patriot whose hit-and-run tactics helped wear down the enemy during the Revolutionary War died. Abiathar is buried alongside Mary and their daughter and son-in-law in Chapel Cemetery, Sandstone Township.

An important tactic in the guerrilla warfare that Abiathar used was hiding in order to launch surprise attacks. The legacy of the Patriot described in the next chapter also involved hiding but for an entirely different purpose. Read on to find out more about his fascinating story.

Chapter 13

DAVID McGEE

Born to: Thomas and Ann (Stewart) McGee on February 14, 1760
Birthplace: Colrain, Massachusetts
Moved to: Concord Township in 1833 at seventy-three years
Died: December 3, 1852
Burial: Maple Grove Cemetery, Concord Township

Young David McGee had no idea that his heartfelt yearning for freedom would affect him so personally or that it would ripple through multiple generations, inspiring his descendants to put their lives on the line for those seeking freedom from slavery. But such is the case for this Revolutionary War Patriot, whose impact stretched far beyond his life.

David, the son of Thomas and Ann (Stewart) McGee, was born in Colrain, Massachusetts, on what today is celebrated as Valentine's Day—February 14, 1760. He first enlisted with the local militia in March 1777 at the age of seventeen. During his multiple tours of service, he stood guard during the icy winter at Fort Ticonderoga, New York, to prevent the British from crossing the frozen lake and launching a surprise attack.

As an example of how severe some winters were during the Revolutionary War, the "hard winter" of 1779–80 was so frigid that every water inlet from North Carolina to Canada froze over completely. One source reported that some snowfalls dropped more than four feet of snow, with snowdrifts over six feet. Temperatures only made it above freezing a couple times in the whole winter. Officers even remembered ink freezing in their quill pens.

The Enduring Dream of Freedom

Revolutionary War Patriot David McGee (1760–1852) passed on more than a surname to his offspring. Descendants alive in the mid-1800s also inherited his fierce love of freedom. David's son Thomas McGee (1790–1869) and his grandson Melville McGee (1828–1909) both participated in a clandestine system that transported freedom seekers from slave states in the South to free states in the North and Canada from about 1830 to 1865. The system, known as the Underground Railroad, was secret because it was against the law to aid and assist in the escape of an enslaved person. Not only did David's homestead serve as a hiding place for freedom seekers, but McGee descendants helped transport enslaved persons to the next stop along the line.

Was David among soldiers who recalled such things? And what impact did the elements have on this teen as he stood guard outside during a stinging cold winter? Those personal details are unknown, but it is known that David also participated in the Battle of Stillwater (Saratoga County, New York, September 20, 1777), which led to the surrender of British General John Burgoyne—a pivotal Patriot victory that helped turn the tide of the war.

In 1783, David married his first wife, who died shortly thereafter. His second wife, however, Mary Kendall (1768–1853), was a lifelong companion. The couple had several children. David worked as a tanner and shoemaker, according to a descendant who was quoted in a local newspaper article. Over the years, the McGees felt the pull to travel westward, and in 1833, the family moved from Warren County, New York, to Concord Township, where they are credited as being among the first settlers.

Seven years later, at the age of eighty, the Revolutionary War Patriot appeared before the Circuit Court of Jackson to seek his war pension. His application was certified by court clerk William R. DeLand, who, in a harbinger of things to come, was one of the leaders in Jackson's Underground Railroad network, a secret system that helped to transport freedom seekers from slave states in the South to free states in the North, Canada and other countries.

While William certified that David had indeed appeared before the clerk as required, the government ultimately did not approve David's pension

DAR To Designate Grave at C

Jackson Women's Calendar

By DENISE R. BELCHER

David McGee's Revolutionary War record went unrecognized by the Department of the Army during his life, and for more than the first 100 years after his death. But Tuesday, Sarah Treat Prudden Chapter, Daughters of the American Revolution, plans to give him his due.

The group will dedicate a bronze marker it purchased to attach to his gravestone, declaring his part in the formation of the United States, during the country's Fourth of July birthday celebration.

Descendants of the soldier who expect to attend the ceremony include a great-great-granidson, Walter K. McGee, 1111 S. Webster; his sister, Mrs. John G. Rossiter of Dexter, the former Ruth McGee and another great-great-granddaughter, Mrs. Leonard H. Field III, 2010 Glen, the former Janet McGee.

Walter McGee's daughter, Miss Mary A. McGee of Lansing, plans to read her ancestor's service record during the rites in Maple Grove Cemetery

TRACERS—Mrs. John F. Haughey, 515 Garfield, and Mrs. Floyd Lyke of Wolf Lake, members of Sarah Treat Prudden Chapter, DAR, consult with Natalie and Harriet Field, 2010 Glen, about the Revolutionary War record of their great-great-great-grandfather, David McGee. (CP Photo)

Top, left: This is the grave monument for Patriot David McGee, who is buried in Maple Grove Cemetery, Concord Township. *Courtesy Linda Hass.*

Top, right: This plaque was placed on the headstone of Patriot David McGee by Jackson's Sarah Treat Prudden Chapter National Society Daughters of the American Revolution. *Courtesy Linda Hass.*

Bottom: This article in the July 2, 1967 *Jackson Citizen Patriot* shows descendants of Patriot David McGee reviewing his Revolutionary War record. *Courtesy Jackson Public Library.*

application since he did not serve the minimum six months total. David's response shows the magnanimity of his character: "I cheerfully comply with your directions. I am respectfully your obedient servant."

The respectful Patriot who found the perfect balance between being a patriotic warrior and an obedient servant died on December 3, 1852, at the age of ninety-two and was buried in Maple Grove Cemetery, Concord Township. Multiple generations of McGees have since been buried in Maple Grove Cemetery, including David's second wife, Mary, who died in 1853, and their son, Thomas McGee (1790–1869).

The McGee family's participation in the Underground Railroad illustrates, among other things, the importance of livestock for transportation during the eighteenth and nineteenth centuries. In his case, horses were used to pull wagons that transported freedom seekers (see "The Enduring Dream of Freedom"). The next story highlights another vital—and some would say life-sustaining—use of livestock during the Revolutionary War.

Chapter 14

JABEZ MOSHER JR.

Born to: Jabez Mosher Sr. and Elizabeth (Preston) Mosher on March 16, 1759
Birthplace: Quaker Hill, New York
Moved to: Brooklyn, Columbia Township in or before 1851
at eighty to ninety years
Died: October 27, 1851
Burial: Mount Evergreen Cemetery, City of Jackson

Of the many services that a Revolutionary War soldier could render, herding cattle is probably not one that readily comes to mind, yet this was one of the tasks assigned to Patriot Jabez Mosher Jr., a private with the New York Militia.

Jabez, a New York resident, enlisted with his father's militia company in 1776 at the age of seventeen. During the teenager's multiple tours, which extended to 1779, he helped apprehend British Loyalists, reinforce Continental forces at various forts and conduct scouting expeditions along the frontier, and he participated in several conflicts, including the Battle of Monmouth (New Jersey, 1778).

But his most unusual assignment was driving a herd of cattle from Fort Edward, New York, to Bennington, Vermont, a distance of about fifty miles (see "Cattle Drives and the Revolutionary War"). If Jabez's duties were similar to other herd drivers at the time, he spent many sleepless nights watching the herd, scaring off predators and enduring the open elements—from blazing sun to blinding blizzards. He also was vigilant about protecting

DEATHS

At Brooklyn, October 26th. of Old Age, Mr. JABEZ MOSHER, aged 94 years.

The deceased was Father of B. G. Mosher of Brooklyn, and through a long life had borne an unblemished character for integrity and usefulness. During the Revolutionary struggle, Mr. Mosher served his country faithfully to the end of the War, and was a participant in several Battles, among which were those of Monmouth, and Brandywine. Peace to his ashes. COM.

Above: This obituary for Patriot Jabez Mosher, published in the November 19, 1851 *American Citizen* newspaper, praised his Revolutionary War service. *Courtesy Jackson District Library.*

Left: This is the grave monument for Patriot Jabez Mosher, who is buried in Mount Evergreen Cemetery, Jackson. *Courtesy Linda Hass.*

Cattle Drives and the Revolutionary War

Providing life-sustaining food for hungry troops has always been essential, but in the 1700s, the task was complicated by the lack of refrigeration and competition from British foragers. At one point early in 1778, when General George Washington's army was encamped in Valley Forge, Pennsylvania, he sent several hundred troops to New Jersey (known as the "Breadbasket of the Revolution") to collect cattle. The troops found 150 head, and since horses and wagons were in short supply for transporting butchered beef, the troops drove the cattle to Valley Forge. The life-sustaining beef and hides that resulted from this drive likely helped to keep many starving and shoeless Continental soldiers alive.

the cattle from poachers, usually Loyalists attempting to steal cattle from colonial farmers in order to sell the beef to the British.

In 1782, Jabez married his first wife, Abagail/Abigail Deake (1765–1828), in his home state of New York. The couple had many children, at least one of whom is buried in Jackson County. Abigail died in 1828. In 1832, seventy-three-year-old Jabez filed for his pension, which was approved.

In 1834, Jabez married his second wife, Mariah Belay/Beley (1785–1863), in New York. Not much is known about Mariah, including where she is buried, but it is known that the couple had no children. On or before 1851, Jabez moved to Brooklyn, Columbia Township, to be near his son Benjamin Mosher (1809–1874, buried in Mount Evergreen Cemetery).

On October 27, 1851, the Patriot who once drove cattle to feed hungry soldiers passed away at the age of ninety-two. His obituary in the November 19, 1851 *American Citizen* praised Jabez with these words: "The deceased… had borne an unblemished character for integrity and usefulness. During the Revolutionary struggle, Mr. Mosher served his country faithfully to the end of the War, and was a participant in several battles….Peace to his ashes." The Patriot who was willing to do anything for his country—including drive cattle—is buried in Mount Evergreen Cemetery, Jackson.

Jabez's story illustrates, among other things, the need for soldiers to endure the open elements, from the extreme heat of summer to icy winters. The next Patriot not only endured the elements but also walked "on" them in a mission that was likely frightening but also stirring.

Chapter 15

ABRAHAM OSBORN(E)

Born to: Unknown
Birthplace: Morristown, New Jersey, 1755
Moved to: Michigan around 1837, in his eighties
Died: circa 1841–43
Burial: Headstone in Cement City Cemetery, Columbia Township

Many Michiganders can identify with walking on a frozen body of water, especially since our Great Lakes State is also known as a "Winter Wonderland." Those who have ventured on the ice likely also can recall having a slightly queasy feeling, wondering how long the ice would hold their weight and how deep the lake was.

That same feeling no doubt passed through Patriot Abraham Osborn's mind as his New York Militia crossed the frozen Hudson River in the winter of 1775. Abraham, of New York, had joined the militia in December 1775 at the age of twenty. Did he hear a crack or two under his feet during this icy sojourn? Was the ice clear enough for him to see the river's bottom, and was it deep in spots? One thing is certain: his militia trudged on unwaveringly toward its destination—Fort Constitution, New Castle, New Hampshire. The militia was ordered there to join other troops in defending the fortification against any advancing British troops. Since the weather was cold enough to freeze a river, it was undoubtedly miserable in a fort heated only by campfires and fireplaces.

Abraham survived the winter and remained at the fort until March 1776, when he was discharged. The following summer, he reenlisted with the militia, which was sent to Kings Bridge in Bronx, New York, to help construct several cheval-de-frise. These vital defensive barriers were usually placed atop or around earthworks constructed outside the fort and were also known as "redoubts." They allowed soldiers to fire on the enemy outside the fort and still be protected. Larger cheval-de-frise were also employed as underwater obstructions whose larger spikes were designed to prevent ships from continuing passage up rivers.

After completing this task, his regiment was assigned to Peekskill, New York, where Abraham remained until his term expired in January 1777, having served in the American Revolution for a total of eight months.

Sometime after the war, Abraham married Loretta Finch (1762–1841) in New York. The couple, who remained in that state for several decades, had several children. Abraham applied for his pension in June 1833 at the age of seventy-eight. Two fellow Patriots, Ebenezer Bartlett and Anthony Swartout, submitted statements in support of the application. Ebenezer recalled serving with Abraham for an additional month at Fort Constitution in January 1776, and Anthony Swartout stated he served in the same company as Abraham and that they marched together to King's Bridge. Abraham's pension was approved in May 1834 and backdated to March 1834.

The Interesting Epitaph of Loretta Osborn

The epitaph on the headstone of Loretta Osborn, wife of Patriot Abraham Osborn, describes an interesting chapter in American history. It states, "Loretta Finch Osborn figured in the Wyoming NY massacre. She and her little brother were taken captives by the Indians after their father was killed and scalped." According to Osborn descendants, the massacre took place in an area now known as Wilkes-Barre, Pennsylvania. During the attack, young Loretta was captured with her six-year-old brother, Asahel. To prevent her brother from being killed, she carried him for many miles to keep pace with the fast-moving warriors. Ultimately, she went on to rejoin settlers, marry Abraham Osborn and become part of the fascinating history of American Revolutionary War figures with headstones in Jackson County.

This is the grave monument for Patriot Abraham Osborn, who is buried in the Cement City Cemetery, Columbia Township. *Courtesy Linda Hass.*

Around 1837, the eighty-two-year-old Patriot moved to Michigan to reside with son Samuel and his family in Woodstock, Lenawee County, and in March 1837, Abraham requested that his pension be transferred to Lenawee County. Another son, Jesse Osborn, lived in nearby Tecumseh.

After several years in his new home state, the Revolutionary War Patriot who walked on frozen rivers and once built defensive fortifications was laid to rest in either 1841 or 1843, in his eighties. But Abraham's path to remembrance was far from over. It has long puzzled history buffs why he and his wife are listed as buried in Lenawee County yet have headstones in Cement City, Jackson County.

Recently discovered archival newspaper articles and related documents shed light on this curious contradiction. When the puzzle pieces are assembled, a picture emerges showing that Abraham and Loretta were originally buried on the Osborn farm in Woodstock, Lenawee County. Their burial site, formerly an orchard, was inadvertently plowed over in the early 1900s by the property owner at that time, farmer Henry C. Allen. If the Osborns' grave markers were of wood or soft stone such as sandstone, these memorials likely no longer existed or were not readily visible when Allen set his plow to the earth decades later. Once the site was tilled, neither Osborn descendants nor experts could relocate the original burial site.

One article stated that Allen offered to have a burial monument placed on his property in the approximate spot of the Osborn graves. But Osborn descendants and the former Homer-based Daughters of the American Revolution, which took an interest in the incident, feared a future farmer might make the same mistake, so they obtained monuments for both Abraham and Loretta Osborn and placed them in the Cement City Cemetery, Columbia Township. Jackson County was likely chosen because several Osborn descendants lived in Jackson at the time. An unveiling ceremony was held at the Cement City Cemetery on May 22, 1926, and while Abraham and Loretta are not buried there, their monuments help to perpetuate the memory of one of America's original defenders in a tangible way that brings comfort to his descendants and stands as an enduring testament to Abraham's service.

Like Abraham, the Patriot described in the next chapter also served multiple tours. Among his sources of inspiration were family members whose revolutionary zeal burned brightly.

Chapter 16

ADAM OVERACKER (OVEROCKER)

Born to: Michael and Anna (Stober/Stover) Overacker on June 27, 1761
Birthplace: Beekman Precinct, New York
Moved to: southern Michigan circa 1833 in his seventies
Died: November 14, 1842
Burial: Grass Lake East Cemetery, Grass Lake Township

For many American families, the Revolutionary War was a time of division, with some members (Patriots) supporting independence for a fledgling America and others (Loyalists) supporting Great Britain. America's founding fathers were no exception—Patriots Benjamin Franklin, Thomas Jefferson and John Hancock all had relatives who backed the British cause.

For Adam Overacker, however, joining the revolutionary cause was a family affair. His father, Michael Overacker, served on a Committee of Correspondence—that is, an emergency provisional group that helped to organize and mobilize resistance to British forces in communities throughout the original thirteen colonies. Other family members serving in Adam's militia included George Overacker, Jacob Overacker and Michael Overacker, who may have been Adam's father or another relative. Regardless, there was no doubt where the Overacker family stood when it came to freedom and independence.

Adam's multiple tours began in the fall of 1777, when the sixteen-year-old served as a minuteman with the New York Militia. His unit was called to serve in the Saratoga Campaign, a major conflict climaxing with the Battle of Saratoga (Saratoga, New York, fall 1777). During the battle, Patriot troops won a decisive victory that fueled revolutionary determination.

During Adam's deployments with other militias from 1778 to 1782, his units continued to reinforce Continental troops and perform vital duties such as cutting and rafting timber. To perform this task, Adam and other soldiers cut trees and dropped logs in the river. The logs were then connected by rope to rafts, which Adam and others used to guide the wooden flotilla to their destination downstream. On land, the crew used the lumber to build structures in the fort, from barracks to bunk beds. This job was particularly important because Fort Edward was a vital Patriot stronghold in Washington County, New York.

Adam's personal life had multiple chapters as well, with many pages bearing witness to the challenges and mortality rates that plagued Americans in the post-Revolutionary era. Adam married his first wife, Cornelia VanderCook/Vandercook, in 1781, while he was a twenty-year-old serving in the militia. The couple had several children, at least one of whom moved to Grass Lake

During the Revolutionary War, lumber was vital in constructing forts, from barracks to bunkbeds. *Photo by Linda Hass, courtesy #thisismackinac.*

This photo illustrates the various uses for lumber in a typical Revolutionary War fort. *Photo by Linda Hass, courtesy #thisismackinac.*

This is the grave monument for Patriot Adam Overacker, who is buried in East Grass Lake Cemetery, Grass Lake Township. *Courtesy Linda Hass.*

The Curious Facts About Adam Overacker

The birth date on Adam's grave marker—1759—appears to be incorrect. His military and other records consistently record a birth year of 1761. Another curious fact is that Adam is the second Revolutionary War Patriot, in addition to David McGee, who had connections with the Underground Railroad. Adam's son-in-law, Henry A. Francisco, was a well-known operative for the secret network, which was in operation during the later part of Adam's life.

Township and is buried there. Cornelia died around 1810 at about forty-nine in either New York or Cuyahoga County, Ohio.

Sometime after this, Adam moved to Ohio, where he married his second wife, widow Chloe Canfield Burke, in 1826 at the age of sixty-five. The couple then moved to Michigan. Chloe died after only seven years of marriage and is buried in southeastern Michigan. The couple had no children.

In 1833, Adam, then seventy-two, married his third and last wife, widow Patience Harrington Adams (1774–1872), in Monroe County, Michigan. The couple resided in Adam's home in Washtenaw County. That same year, Adam's pension was granted. He had applied for his pension in 1832 while a resident of Saline, Michigan, stating that he served no less than three years total. His certificate, issued on August 9, 1833, granted him eighty dollars per year.

It's likely that Adam and Patience moved one last time in 1842 to Grass Lake Township, to be near Adam's daughter, Catherine (Overacker) Francisco, based on his burial site in that township. On November 14, 1842, the eighty-one-year-old Patriot who participated in one of the most pivotal battles of the Revolution and helped to build barracks at Fort Edward breathed his last, ending the last chapter of his long life. He was buried in Grass Lake East Cemetery, Grass Lake Township, where he shares a large granite marker with his daughter, Catherine Francisco (1796–1851), and her husband, Henry A. Francisco. Henry Francisco was also a veteran of the War of 1812, which was often referred to as the Second American Revolution.

Patience Overacker Overocker, who received the pension allowed for Revolutionary War widows, died in 1872 at the incredible age of ninety-

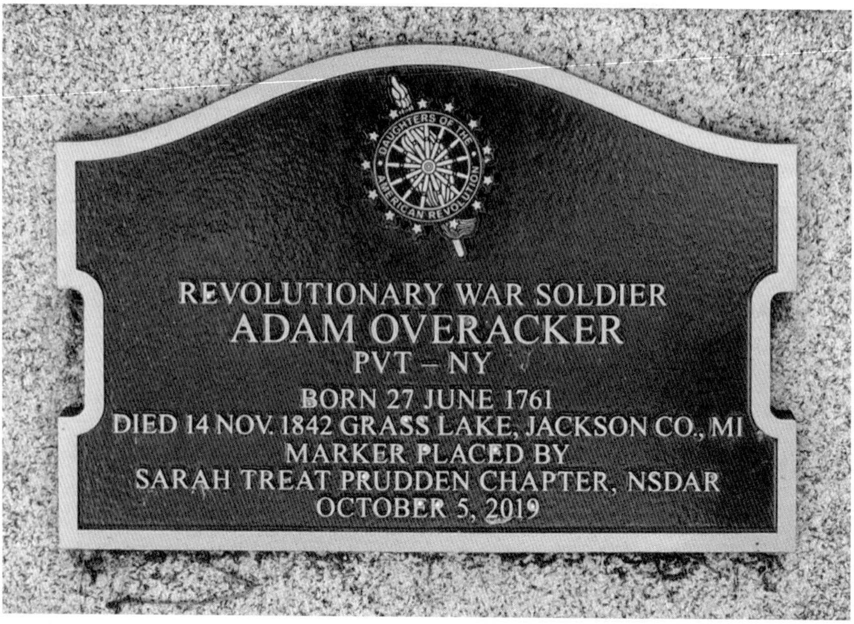

This plaque was placed on the headstone of Patriot Abraham Overacker by the Sarah Treat Prudden Chapter National Society Daughters of the American Revolution. *Courtesy Linda Hass.*

eight. She was likely buried in Grass Lake Township (the exact place is unconfirmed).

Like Adam, the Patriot described in the next chapter also enlisted in the local militia at sixteen. But not only was he fighting for his new homeland—he was fighting for his literal home!

Chapter 17

JOHN PERRIN(E)

Born to: Henry and Mary (La Rue) Perrine, July 22, 1760
Birthplace: Freehold, New Jersey
Moved to: Sandstone Township in or before 1831 in his seventies
Died: December 1831
Burial: Dearing Cemetery, Sandstone Township

New Jersey Patriot John Perrine had very personal reasons to join the fight for independence against the British. Certainly, the cause of liberty was a motivating factor; but at one point in the Revolutionary War, he and his brother were also fighting for their literal home. John was born in Freehold, New Jersey, in 1760. He was the son of French Huguenots—that is, French Protestants who fled religious persecution in France. Many Huguenots, including ancestors of Jackson's DeLand family, immigrated to America and brought with them a fierce love of freedom.

About a year after the Revolutionary War began, John enlisted with the local militia at the age of sixteen. He fought at various times with both infantry and dragoon (cavalry) units from 1777 to 1780. The war became very personal for John, however, when the family's farm was caught in the crossfire during the Battle of Monmouth Courthouse (New Jersey, June 1778). Both John and his brother, Lewis, fought in the battle, which caused extensive damage to their house and orchard. Historians say the conflict resulted in a draw, but the good news for John was that, when the dust settled, the Patriot side retained possession of the battlefield—including the Perrine home.

The Whiskey Rebellion of 1794

The Whiskey Rebellion of 1794 was an uprising of farmers and distillers in western Pennsylvania who protested a whiskey tax enacted by the federal government to help fund the fledgling government. Following years of aggression with tax collectors, the region finally exploded in a confrontation that resulted in President Washington sending in troops to quell what some feared could become a full-blown revolution. New Jersey resident John Perrine, who was buried in Sandstone Township, was among the soldiers called up. The Whiskey Rebellion is considered one of the first major tests of the authority of the newly formed U.S. government. Interestingly, this is the only time in American history that a sitting president physically led U.S. military forces as the commander-in-chief.

John described the day of the battle as the hottest he had ever experienced in his life, and he recalled seeing fourteen British soldiers dead from heat prostration alongside a nearby brook. Historians describe the day as "sweltering" and say that several dozen died from heat stroke alone. One can imagine that a militia man, unencumbered by the layers of an official uniform and able to take cover in the shadows, would fare better than British soldiers marching in full uniform.

After the Revolution, thirty-four-year-old John continued to serve in the New Jersey Militia from September to December 1794. In fact, John's militia was among many called by President George Washington to suppress a domestic rebellion caused by whiskey producers who not only refused to pay tax on their product but also initiated violent demonstrations in protest of the tax (see "Whiskey Rebellion 1794"). This mini-rebellion after the Revolution was the first major test of the new government.

En route to suppress the uprising with his unit, John became ill in Pittsburgh, where he remained until the army returned. Afterward, President Washington visited the militia's sick and wounded and stopped by John's bedside. Before President Washington departed, John recalled Washington's exact words to him: "I hope by Divine Providence you may recover." It is interesting to speculate how many of Jackson's historic figures could say they had conversed with President Washington personally—likely, not many.

John Perrine's unit helped to dispel a mini rebellion over taxation on whiskey, which was often stored in barrels like this. *Photo by Linda Hass, courtesy #thisismackinac.*

This is the grave monument for Patriot John Perrine, who is buried in Dearing Cemetery, Sandstone Township. *Courtesy Linda Hass.*

In 1781, John married his first wife, Catherine/Catharine Williamson (1759–1792), in New Jersey. Of the couple's surviving children, one is buried in Jackson County. Catherine died at the tender age of thirty-three in 1792 and is buried in New Jersey. One year later, John married Mary Ely of Freehold, New Jersey. The couple had several children. It appears that none from this second marriage are buried in Jackson County.

In 1798, the Perrine family moved to Lyons, New York. John's occupations in New York before 1825 are unknown, but that year, he was among many workers who helped to build the Erie Canal, which at that time was 365 miles long. This architectural wonder was the first navigable waterway linking the Atlantic Ocean to the Great Lakes—a flowing connector that spurred westward movement of American settlers.

Interestingly, the Erie Canal was built before dynamite was used to help laborers blast through stubborn rock and before steam-powered earth-movers and excavators were used to clear mud, rock and rubble. Instead, the rocky, thickly forested land was cleared and the forty-foot-wide canal was dug by the raw manpower of an estimated fifty thousand laborers. Since sixty-five-year-old John was among the laborers, it's obvious this Patriot was still a man of strength and stamina.

Sometime in or before 1831, John moved to Sandstone Township to be near his eldest son, Henry Perrine (1786–1853, buried in Dearing Cemetery, Sandstone Township). Mary's date of death and burial location have not been confirmed, but documents show that John was a widower by this time. In December 1831, the seventy-one-year-old Patriot who fought for his homeland and literal home in New Jersey—and who was among the privileged few to meet General Washington personally—breathed his last. John Perrine is buried in Dearing Cemetery, Sandstone Township, with his son Henry Perrine.

The Patriot described in the next chapter also witnessed a personal exchange involving General Washington; however, this exchange was not as pleasant as John's. Read on to find out more about this heated confrontation between Washington and one of his commanders.

Chapter 18

ISAAC QUIGLEY

Born to: Isaac and Mary Quigley,
on February 3, 1763
Birthplace: Nottingham, Burlington County, New Jersey (now in Mercer County)
Moved to: Napoleon Township circa 1837 at seventy-four years
Died: September 10, 1850
Burial: Mount Hope Cemetery, Waterloo Township

When most people think of "teamsters," they imagine truck drivers barreling down a highway. But did you know that teamsters played a crucial role in the American Revolution? Obviously, they didn't drive motorized vehicles, but they did use horsepower to transport cargo that included such essential supplies as guns, ammunition and food to Patriot troops.

Isaac Quigley, of Irish ancestry and born in Nottingham Township, New Jersey, was one of those early teamsters. His involvement with the New Jersey Militia began the morning of June 26, 1778, when he was plowing his family's New Jersey cornfield. The lad heard gunfire and saw smoke and ran to the alarm post located near the residence of his uncle, Captain Robert Quigley. Alarm posts, nondescript rallying points where minutemen assembled, were often located near large trees; hence the preservation and care of "liberty trees" throughout New England. At the post, Isaac received a written order directing him to tell men in the community to appear for service.

This is the grave monument for Patriot Isaac Quigley, who is buried in Mount Hope Cemetery, Waterloo Township. *Courtesy Linda Hass.*

Not only did he follow through, the fifteen-year-old also joined the militia as a private in his uncle's company that same day. Although Isaac did not meet the age requirement of sixteen, this rule was often overlooked in times of emergency. Thus began several tours of duty from 1778 to 1781, in which Isaac's units were deployed throughout New Jersey, Pennsylvania, Maryland and Virginia. His service included guarding warehouses for the American army, making embankments, breaking up Tory smuggling rings and reinforcing other militias.

The teen also witnessed and wrote about the famous confrontation between General George Washington and Charles Lee, commander of Washington's advance guard. Isaac noted in his pension application that the confrontation was sparked when Washington asked Lee why he ordered his men to retreat from advancing British forces during the Battle of Monmouth (New Jersey, June 28, 1778). Lee's audible reply—that his soldiers lacked "fortitude"—rankled nearby soldiers, one of whom uttered that Lee's answer was a "damnable lie." Isaac, who noted the exchange in his pension report, wrote that he agreed and that other soldiers also were willing to go forward.

Apparently, Washington felt the same way. He reprimanded Lee in front of his men. Then Washington ordered Lee to re-form the men for an attack. The conflict (also called "Battle of Monmouth Courthouse") ended in a draw, but Patriot forces did prevail in retaining possession of the ground.

One of the more interesting aspects of Isaac's service involved serving as a teamster. In Isaac's case, he used his father's horse-drawn wagon to convey wood and hay to Patriot forces at different locations. This transportation service was essential in sustaining troops and keeping the army well equipped with various supplies, including hay to feed horses and campfire wood for cooking and warmth.

After the war, Isaac returned home with little more than the clothes on his back and a promissory of future payment for his services. He was not alone. Most veterans had only paper IOUs, which many soldiers sold at reduced rates in order to get cash for immediate needs such as food and clothing (see "The Fate of the Returning Soldier"). Even so, Isaac eked out a living, likely on his father's farm.

In 1790, Isaac married Amy Gale (1768–1848). The couple lived in several New England states and had many children, at least two of whom are buried in Jackson County. Around 1837, the government gave seventy-four-year-old Isaac a land grant for property in Michigan, likely in lieu of payment. Isaac and his family moved to Michigan and claimed land in Napoleon Township, but they never escaped poverty.

THE FATE OF THE RETURNING SOLDIER

When the Revolutionary War ended in 1783, many soldiers returned home with little more than their worn clothes and promissory notes from a government that lacked funds to pay them. Not only did fighting in the eight-year war mean lost time in regard to developing job opportunities or employable skills, but several Patriots were unable to work because of injuries. Widows were impacted, too, since many lost their bread earners and had hungry mouths to feed. As a result, in 1818, Congress passed the first veterans' pension legislation. This act had such stringent requirements that most applicants were ineligible. It wasn't until 1832 that Congress passed a more all-encompassing pension act. Over the next few decades, over eighty thousand people, including men and women, applied for pension benefits.

In March 1847, Isaac applied to the government for a pension, stating he and his wife were "destitute." He included statements from community members who testified to Isaac's veracity and his reputation as a Patriot. The government denied his application for many reasons, including lack of "proper documentation." In July 1847, Isaac applied again, only to receive another denial.

In 1848, Isaac's wife died. One year later, his son Isaac Quigley Jr. died. The 1850 U.S. census shows that the eighty-seven-year-old widower lived with the Arnold family in rural Leoni Township that year. It is not known why Isaac didn't stay with his other son Samuel Quigley, who lived in nearby Waterloo Township. Perhaps the Arnolds were a family connection on Isaac's wife's side, or maybe the Arnolds could afford to take in another mouth to feed.

Regardless, on September 10, 1850, poverty ended for the former teamster who risked his life to provide essential supplies for Patriot troops. Isaac Quigley, eighty-seven, was buried in Mount Hope Cemetery, Waterloo Township. His son Samuel Quigley (1792–1860) also was buried in the same cemetery a decade later. The son who preceded him in death, Isaac Quigley Jr. (1799–1849), was buried in Norvell Cemetery, Norvell Township. It is not known where Amy Quigley was buried, but it was likely in Jackson County.

Isaac's story is a poignant reminder that not all stories end happily for these first veterans who gave their all for their fledgling country. It also sheds light on the sacrifices Patriots made and the corresponding hardships that followed many Patriots for the rest of their lives.

While Isaac fought against British forces on the battlefield, the Patriot described in the next chapter was among a select group who fought the British with their eyes and ears—as spies!

Chapter 19

THOMAS SWARTOUT

Born to: Thomas and Judith (Hill) Swartout on March 2, 1753
Birthplace: Fishkill, New York
Moved to: Brooklyn circa 1837, at about eighty-four years of age
Died: September 12, 1848
Burial: Cement City Cemetery, Columbia Township

One of the many intriguing chapters of the Revolutionary War was the role that spies played in gathering information on the enemy's plans and whereabouts. Thomas Swartout, a Fishkill, New York native, was among this secretive corps of Patriot spies who gathered and carried vital intelligence about the British.

From 1776 to 1779, Thomas volunteered to serve various tours of duty, from one to several months at a time. During his tours as a twenty-three- to twenty-six-year-old, his units helped provide security for New York's Third Provincial Congress; protect Patriot civilians from raids conducted by marauding British Loyalists; construct forts; and assist desperate colonists whose homes had been burned.

Most of the time, however, Thomas was engaged in monitoring the travels of the British army, tracking the movements of British ships and gathering and carrying secret intelligence on activities occurring between White Plains, New York, and New York City—a distance of about thirty miles (see "Washington's Spies"). While spies' methods were not as sophisticated as they are today, they did involve some creative practices, such as writing in invisible ink.

Washington's Spies

In 1775, when the Second Continental Congress chose George Washington as commander-in-chief of the Continental armies, Washington organized a spy network whose methods included writing letters in invisible ink and even airing colored laundry. The latter example involved a female agent named Anna Strong who lived on the coast in Setauket, New York. Her job was to relay signals to Patriot couriers smuggling intelligence. According to historians, she hung out different types of laundry on a clothesline—in full view of British soldiers and also of boats moving through the sound. If she hung a black petticoat, that signaled that a message was ready to be picked up by a Patriot courier. She would then hang handkerchiefs, the number of which would correspond to a secret pickup spot.

Both Patriot and British armies relied on male and female spies to gather information on troop strength, the availability of supplies and adversaries' plans to march or attack. One can only imagine the risks Thomas took in obtaining and passing on this vital and secret information, whether donning a disguise or stealthily moving from one place to another under the cover of darkness (see "Women in the American Revolution").

After the war, Thomas married Judith Hill. The couple, who resided in Olive, New York, had many children. In 1832, at the age of seventy-nine, Thomas filed for a pension, which was granted. In the mid- to late 1830s, three of the couple's children moved to Jackson County. Sometime between 1835 and 1836, Judith died, and on October 13, 1837, Thomas, an aging widower, requested that his pension be transferred to a post office in Brooklyn, Columbia Township, which was near his children.

A descendant quoted in a local newspaper article shed more light on the impetus for Thomas's move to Jackson. According to the article, the Patriot was given a one-thousand-acre "land grant" in Jackson County during the presidency of Martin Van Buren (eighth president of the United States, 1837–41).

Thomas spent eleven more years in his new residence and would have witnessed vital stages in the township's development. He was already there when Columbia Township was officially established in 1838, and he might

Marker-Placing Ceremony Is Held by D. A. R. at Grave Of Revolutionary Soldier

Of interest to the residents of Jackson was the ceremony held Tuesday at the grave of Thomas Swartout in Cement City when a marker was placed on the final resting place of this soldier in the Revolutionary War.

Mr. Swartout died 75 years ago but it was not until the past week that public recognition was given his part in the battle for the independence of this country. On Tuesday his descendants, friends and 30 representatives of Charity Cook Chapter, Daughters of the American Revolution of Homer, gathered around his grave, placed an appropriately lettered marker thereon and with public exercises paid tribute to the memory of a 91 years, and Andrew Swartout, aged 86, great, great grandsons of the soldier whose memory was being honored. The two great, great grandsons of the revolutionary soldier are shown in the accompanying picture, Andrew being on the left, with the great, great, great grandson, Lewis Akin, between them.

Climbers Will Try Again to Scale World's Highest Peak

London, June 30.—Although last year's attempt to reach the summit of Mount Everest failed, the Royal Geographical Society intends

Left: This is the grave monument for Patriot Thomas Swartout in Cement City Cemetery, Columbia Township. *Courtesy Linda Hass.*

Right: This article described the ceremony honoring Patriot Thomas Swartout, held by his descendants and the Daughters of the American Revolution. *Courtesy Jackson District Library archives.*

have marveled at the township's expansion to 1,560 people by 1839, including expanding settlements in Brooklyn and Jefferson, among locations.

On September 12, 1848, the soldier who once built forts, protected civilians and spied on behalf of his country died at the age of ninety-five. It is not known where Judith is buried, but Thomas is buried in the Cement City Cemetery, Columbia Township, near his children Andrew Swartout (1790–1859), James Swartout (1792–1847) and Mary "Polly" (Swartout) Cary (1797–1885).

Either his original grave marker did not withstand the elements very well or it did not mention his military service, because in 1923, the Charity Cook Chapter National Society Daughters of the American Revolution provided a new marker that identified him as a Revolutionary War Patriot. The marker, unveiled in a ceremony honoring Thomas's service, also was attended by many Swartout descendants.

Women in the American Revolution

While it's true that the American Revolutionary War was waged mostly by men, it's also true that women played important roles in our country's struggle for freedom, serving as spies, nurses in military camps and organizers of fundraisers. They also produced home-spun materials for clothing and other needs, and at least one served as a soldier. One of the most dramatic episodes was Massachusetts native Deborah Sampson (1760–1827). Deborah disguised herself as a man named Robert Shurtleff (Shurtliff) and fought for seventeen months before her gender was revealed due to medical treatment. She is the only woman to earn a full military pension for participation in the Revolutionary army. Women are still making contributions to the American Revolutionary cause today through such organizations as the National Society Daughters of the American Revolution. To learn more about this worthwhile organization, see the appendix titled "Resources."

While spies had various methods of sending and receiving coded signals in the American Revolution, there were other nonverbal cues that also helped to communicate valuable information to Patriot forces—cues that involved music. The next chapter describes the life of a Patriot who was instrumental in relaying those vital signals on the battlefield.

Chapter 20

JONATHAN (JOHN) THOMPSON

Born to: Jeremiah/Robert and Elizabeth Thompson
on April 21, 1762
Birthplace: Norwalk, Connecticut
Moved to: Washtenaw County, Michigan, circa 1833, at seventy-one years
Died: May 1847
Burial: Mount Evergreen Cemetery, City of Jackson

One of the most iconic images of the American Revolutionary War is that of a young boy and grizzled Patriot resolutely playing their fife and drum on a battlefield strewn with wounded soldiers. The image not only captures the defiant spirit of the war but also reflects an important reality—instruments were vital during warfare.

Patriot Jonathan Thompson understood the importance of this more than most, serving as a fifer throughout his three years of service. When the sixteen-year-old first apprenticed with a skilled tradesman in Fairfield County, Connecticut, however, he had no idea he would end up playing any instrument—let alone serve in the war. But the teen sensed an opportunity to be released from his apprenticeship when his employer, or "master," was drafted in 1778. The industrious lad used the opportunity to propose that he serve in his master's place. His proposal was enthusiastically accepted by Jonathan's master—who also purchased his uniform.

From 1778 to 1781, Jonathan served on various tours as a fifer for the Connecticut Militia, marching to destinations in Connecticut, New York and New Jersey to reinforce troops and perform other duties. Most of the musicians in the Revolutionary War were either young or old because this kind of service was not as physically grueling as other roles. It was, however, vital.

Fifes and drums were used for communication, regimentation and boosting morale in various ceremonies. On the battlefield, musicians had the responsibility of helping keep order and making sure soldiers functioned as a unit. The high-pitched sound of the fife could be heard above the noise of combat and was used as a signal for various commands, including ceasefire. Music was also used to awaken soldiers, assist with marching cadence and even set the rhythm of camp chores, among other uses.

Likely, the tunes that Jonathan played repeatedly during his three years of service were ingrained in his mind, creating a silent but steady rhythm to his life, even after he was discharged from service in December 1781.

Around 1782, Johnathan changed his given name to "John" at the request of an uncle with the same shortened moniker. Also that year, he married his first wife, Katherine/Catharine Hanford Smith, in New York. It is not known how many children the couple had, but it is known that Katherine died in 1791. A year later, John married his second wife, Elizabeth Raymond. It is believed the couple, who lived in New York, had at least four sons: Hiram, William R., Jeremiah and John Jr.

This is the grave marker for Patriot Jonathan Thompson, who is buried in Mount Evergreen Cemetery, Jackson. *Courtesy Linda Hass.*

From Washtenaw to Jackson County

Why would Patriot John Thompson have been buried in Jackson, since it appears he resided in Washtenaw County during his last days? Very likely, the eighty-five-year-old was visiting his son, Jackson resident Jeremiah Thompson, when he died. The family may have decided that rather than take his body back to Ann Arbor, they would buy a plot in the newly established Mount Evergreen Cemetery. Other family members buried in the plot are son Jeremiah Thompson (1807–1885) and those identified only as "Babies Thompson," hinting that young children or grandchildren also lived in Jackson, necessitating a family burial plot. In addition, the very fact that his obituary was published in the Jackson newspaper also indicates a local connection to the Patriot. Mount Evergreen Cemetery counts among those laid to rest there soldiers from various wars, beginning with this, our nation's first war.

In June 1832, at the age of seventy, John applied for a pension, which was granted in April 1833. Shortly thereafter, the family moved to Michigan and settled in Washtenaw County. In November 1832, Elizabeth died. In 1840, John married his third wife, Mary Johnson, in Ann Arbor. The couple had no children, but they did have seven years together before the beat of life stopped for the fifer whose signals once helped keep the beat on the battlefield. John died sometime in May 1847 and is buried in Mount Evergreen Cemetery, Jackson (see "From Washtenaw to Jackson County"). His obituary in the May 25, 1847 *American Citizen* praised the eighty-five-year-old Patriot with these glowing words: "He was a soldier of the Revolution.... He is remarkable and [it is] worthy of note, that he was never known to taste a drop of ardent spirits....His long life may be attributed in part to his temperate habits. How few of the fathers of the Revolution remain! We trust he has gone to his eternal rest, where wars are known no more."

While John served admirably in the Revolutionary War, the Patriot described in the next chapter actually fought in two wars, with the second opportunity occurring when this veteran was in his sixties. Read on to find out more.

Chapter 21

DANIEL THURSTON

Born to: Nathaniel and Miner (Chase) Thurston on August 24, 1752
Birthplace: Newbury, Massachusetts
Moved to: Waterloo Township before May 1850,
around eighty to ninety years old
Died: May 21, 1850
Burial: Mount Pleasant Cemetery, Waterloo Township

Of all the Patriots described in this book, Daniel Thurston is the only one who fought in two separate wars against the British. Daniel, a Patriot from Newbury, Massachusetts, first felt called to join the Massachusetts Militia as a twenty-three-year-old in the spring of 1775, when hundreds of British troops were spotted marching toward Concord and Lexington. The towns, separated by only seven miles in northeastern Massachusetts, were of strategic importance because they served as storage facilities for colonial gunpowder and cannons. Not only did the British hope to steal or destroy these munitions, but they also wanted to capture Patriot leaders in Lexington. The prospect of this threat was the catalyst for Paul Revere's famous ride on April 18, 1775, alerting the countryside, "The Redcoats are coming!"

To defend these towns, thousands of minutemen—including Daniel—were called to action. Although Concord fell to the British, Patriots successfully repelled British forces in Lexington, preventing them from capturing and destroying the stores of gunpower and military equipment

This sketch depicts the ride of Paul Revere to warn colonists of danger before the battles in Lexington and Concord in Massachusetts. *Wikimedia Commons.*

there. Many historians regard the Battle of Lexington (April 19, 1775) as the first major battle of the American Revolutionary War, making it a pivotal point in American history.

This confrontation no doubt provided a very dramatic, and at times deadly, beginning to Daniel's service. What would it have been like to be among the initial responders trying to stop this advancing red tide that threatened to inundate everything in its path? Perhaps like trying to stop a flood? Incredibly, that is what happened. Daniel, who was not deterred by the underdog status of Patriot troops, went on to serve with the militia in April 1778, marching with his unit over 140 miles to reinforce the Northern Army at Saratoga, New York.

Three years before the war officially ended, Daniel married Hannah Hilton in Fitchburg, Massachusetts. The couple, who lived throughout the New England states, had several children, one of whom is buried in Jackson County. More information might have been known about Daniel were it not

for a fire in 1787 that burned not only his house in Scipio, New York, but also all its contents, including family records.

In 1806, the fifty-four-year-old pioneer bought seven hundred acres of land in Aurora, New York. Soon after, he moved his family there, traveling by ox-driven wagons. The family built a log cabin in "what was then a dense forest" and experienced "all the hardships of pioneer life," according to historical sources.

Daniel, a deacon in the Baptist church who later switched to the Universalist denomination, was described as a man "of good disposition and regular habits." If his appearance was like his son Daniel Jr., he would have stood over six feet tall with a dark complexion and dark brown whiskers and eyes.

In 1811, Hannah died. One year later, sons Daniel Jr. and Thomas Thurston served in the War of 1812 (1812–15). This second conflict between the United States and Great Britain was prompted, among other reasons, when the (British) Royal Navy began capturing American ships, apprehending sailors who had once been British subjects and forcing them to work for the British. In addition to maritime skirmishes, battles were also fought on land. In 1813, Thomas was given permission to leave service and return home to his New York shoemaking business if his father, our subject Daniel Sr., would serve as his substitute.

It is not known exactly why Thomas, twenty-seven, would ask this of his sixty-one-year-old father. Perhaps the family was dependent on the shoemaking business for its income and no one else could ply this craft except son Thomas. Or perhaps his father, a new widower, was restless. For whatever reason, the father served as a substitute for his son and once again stepped forward to defend his country against Britain, enabling Thomas to return to his business.

Toward the end of 1813, the war brought additional twists and turns to the Thurston family, beginning with a message Thomas received that his father had been killed in the line of duty and that Buffalo, New York, was besieged by British troops that had destroyed many buildings and ships in the city. To help defend the town, Thomas traveled there in an ox-driven wagon. Amazingly, just as he reached the outskirts of the burning city, he saw his very much alive father among the American troops! The two did not have much time for a reunion or to ponder the prior, inaccurate death notification, choosing instead to venture farther into the burning city and retrieve valuable ammunition abandoned by retreating U.S. forces. They succeeded and presumably returned the munition stashes to U.S. authorities.

America's Second Revolution

In the War of 1812, the United States fought Great Britain for a second time. Causes of the war included British attempts to restrict U.S. trade, the Royal Navy's impressment of American seamen and America's desire to expand its territory. The United States suffered many defeats at the hands of the British over the course of the war, including the capture and burning of the nation's capital, Washington, D.C., in August 1814. Nonetheless, American troops were able to repulse British invasions in New York, Baltimore and New Orleans, boosting national confidence. The ratification of the Treaty of Ghent on February 17, 1815, ended the war and prompted many to refer to the War of 1812 as a "second war of independence."

Left: This is the grave monument for Patriot Daniel Thurston, who is buried in Mount Pleasant Cemetery, Waterloo Township. *Courtesy Linda Hass.*

Below: This plaque was placed on the headstone of Daniel Thurston by Jackson's Sarah Treat Prudden Chapter National Society Daughters of the American Revolution. *Courtesy Linda Hass.*

When the war ended in 1815, Daniel Sr., then sixty-three, divided his large New York farmland among his sons. Sometime before May 1850, the aging Patriot ventured on one last trip, joining son Thomas and his family in moving to Leoni Township, Jackson County.

Although he had been hearty enough to fight in two wars, including one when he was in his sixties, this last move might have proved too much for him. On May 21, 1850, at the age of ninety-seven, the Patriot who had defended his country twice against Britain and who survived an initial false report of his death died for real. Daniel Thurston was buried in Mount Pleasant Cemetery, Waterloo Township. Twenty-two years later, his son Thomas Thurston (1786–1872) was laid to rest beside him.

One of the locations that Daniel helped to defend was New York. As the second-largest colony and possessor of one of the American colonies' most important ports, the state of New York played a major role in the Revolutionary War. More than one-third of the war's battles occurred in New York, with the Continental army holding the vital Hudson River and the British controlling New York City. The Patriot described in the next chapter was sent to this hotspot to head off deadly enemy raids.

Chapter 22

SAMUEL UNDERWOOD

Born to: Samuel Underwood Sr. and Mary (Belden) Underwood
on April 21, 1767
Birthplace: Sandisfield, Massachusetts
Moved to: Leoni Township in 1832 at sixty-five years
Died: February 2, 1864
Burial: Leoni Township Cemetery, Leoni Township

Samuel Underwood's service with the Massachusetts Militia, from July to November 1781, was packed with action that included traveling hundreds of miles to and from the Mohawk Valley, New York; protecting civilians from British forces; and participating in major battles such as the Battle of Johnstown in New York.

This battle, on October 1781, was prompted after British soldiers, Loyalist militia and their Mohawk allies in Mohawk Valley repeatedly raided this area. During the previous year, these raids had destroyed crops before harvest, burned civilian buildings and killed hundreds of settlers. In addition to the human cost, the raids also disrupted vital food sources and supply routes for settlers and Patriot forces.

In response, the governor of New York called for the formation of militias to defend the valley under the direction of Colonel Marinus Willett. Samuel's militia was among those called up to support this defensive action. It is believed Samuel served as a corporal for this militia. Given his young age, however, questions arise about the accuracy of his birth year, his date of service or his rank.

Regardless of his age, his abilities were tested on October 25, 1781, when another British raiding party was spotted heading toward the Mohawk Valley. Samuel's militia and other coalition members responded by successfully blocking the British advance; then they counterattacked, ultimately forcing British forces to retreat.

In light of the shortness of Samuel's service (less than six months total), he was ineligible for a pension, but he had the satisfaction of knowing that the battle he participated in was one of the last major battles in the northern theater of the American Revolutionary War.

Sometime before 1799, Samuel married Lovicy Spelman. Not much is known about her, but it is presumed she died young. In 1799, he married his second wife, Jemima Fletcher (1774–1850). The couple had many children, one of whom is buried in Jackson County. After the Revolutionary War, Samuel served as an ordained Baptist minister (see "Faith and the Revolution"). In general, Baptist preachers of that period were committed to teaching and actively engaged in the spiritual well-being of their congregations. It is not difficult to imagine that this Patriot, whose war experiences required a confident assertiveness, was unafraid to be a bold witness of his faith.

In 1832, when Samuel was sixty-five, the family moved to Leoni Township, Jackson County, to be near their son Eri Eber Underwood (1806–

Faith and the Revolution

While Revolutionary War Patriot Samuel Underwood became an ordained Baptist minister after the war, the seeds of his faith were likely cultivated by the perception of a righteous cause in which smaller colonial forces fought against a larger foe, much like the biblical David and Goliath. Ministers served the American cause in many capacities during the war, including as military chaplains, as penmen for committees of correspondence and as members of state legislatures and constitutional conventions. Some even took up arms. One prominent example, James Caldwell, a Presbyterian minister, rendered material help during a battle. Upon noticing that the company ran out of paper to hold powder in the barrel of a gun, he hurried to a nearby church and procured a pile of hymn books that provided paper for the job.

Left: This is the grave monument of Patriot Samuel Underwood, who is buried in Leoni Township Cemetery, Leoni Township. *Courtesy Linda Hass.*

Below: This plaque was placed on the headstone of Samuel Underwood by Jackson's Sarah Treat Prudden Chapter National Society Daughters of the American Revolution. *Courtesy Linda Hass.*

1881, buried in Leoni Cemetery, Leoni Township). The couple spent the next eighteen years together in their new home. They might have felt the excitement that followed the opening of Leoni Township's first school in 1833 and the construction of the young township's first flour mill (1832–34). Their ability to share those experiences as a couple ended in 1850, however, when Jemima died and was buried in Leoni Cemetery.

Samuel lived as a widower for thirty-two more years, although the details of his sunset years are unknown. On February 2, 1864, just two months shy of his ninety-seventh birthday, this man of the cloth who was unafraid to take up arms on behalf of his country met his maker. He was buried in Leoni Township Cemetery. In June 1930, a headstone provided by the United States government was placed on his grave by the Leoni Township Cemetery Sexton.

Samuel experienced deadly confrontations during his tour of duty, but probably no Patriot described in this book had as many dramatic experiences as the next one, who fought the British on land and sea.

Chapter 23

JOHN WALL

Born to: John and Ruth (Murdock) Wall on February 3, 1759
Birthplace: Nine Partners, New York
Moved to: Sandstone Township in 1837 at seventy-eight years
Died: March 28, 1849
Burial: Chapel Cemetery, Sandstone Township

Of all the Patriots described in this book, none saw more action than John Wall. The Connecticut-based Patriot fought in major battles with the militia, participated in raids as a ranger, helped to capture British vessels with his crew as a sailor and was a prisoner of war for thirteen months. Amazingly, this fearless fighter survived these experiences and lived to the ripe old age of ninety.

John's enlistments, from one to several months between 1776 and 1780, took place throughout Connecticut and New York and on the open seas. His adventures began in July 1776, when the seventeen-year-old enlisted with the Connecticut Militia. This militia was thrust into two battles in New York: the Battle of Throg's Neck (also called the Battle of Pell's Point), in which Patriots delayed British movements long enough for Washington to avoid being surrounded; and the Battle of White Plains. Both battles occurred in October 1776, and both resulted in Patriot losses.

During his second tour, John enlisted with a company of rangers who conducted raids against the British along the east shore of the Hudson River. Their exploits included ambushing a British camp of forty soldiers and capturing British Loyalists in a hideout. During the raid, John discovered silver coins worth forty British pounds, which he turned over to his colonel. As a reward for the money, John was given a quarter share.

On his third tour, John signed on as a sailor. Over the months, he and crew members aboard the Yankee privateer *General Putnam* captured a British merchant vessel loaded with salt (which they sent to Boston) and three British ships. They sent two of the British ships back to Boston for Patriot usage and returned the third ship to England, with all the sailors having signed parole agreements (that is, agreements not to take up arms against the colonies).

John's fourth tour, however, was the most perilous. He reenlisted with his brother James in "whaleboat service." This involved disrupting British foraging parties and conducting raids on British forces. The tables were turned in one raid, however, when British dragoons (a type of cavalrymen) captured five Patriot crew members, including John. For thirteen months, the sailors were held in a British-occupied prison in New York City known as the "Sugar House" (see "Sugar House Not So Sweet for Prisoners").

Conditions in British prisons and prison ships such as the HMS *Jersey* were horrific. Prisoners were often fed soggy, moldy bread infested with worms. Perhaps John was among prisoners who boiled their bread to kill parasites before eating whatever was left. In November 1780, John and the others were released in a prisoner exchange.

John's health suffered greatly during his incarceration, and he became severely underweight. As a testament to his zeal and determination, he reenlisted only one month after his release, in spite of his weakened condition. The highlight of his fifth and final tour involved raiding Fort George, New York, and capturing the forty British soldiers stationed there. What a triumphant note on which to end his service!

After the Revolution, John returned to the sea as a sailor for six to seven years. In 1788, he married Sally Riker/Reiker (1769–1847) of Maine. The couple lived throughout Connecticut and New York and had several children.

Around 1837, John and Sally moved to Jackson County to be near their sons Chester and Joseph Wall, who had moved to the county earlier. In fact, some sources state that Chester was among the first pioneers of Sandstone Township. When quoted in newspaper articles, several children lauded John and Sally for their devotion to God and their active participation in their local Methodist congregation. The couple also instilled in their children a strong sense of civic duty, love of country and the need to make sacrifices for the greater good, the articles stated.

Left: This is the grave monument of Patriot John Wall, who is buried in Chapel Cemetery, Sandstone Township. *Courtesy Linda Hass.*

Below: The Lansing Chapter Daughters of the American Revolution held a grave-marking dedication for Patriot John Wall and his wife, Sally Wall, in a special ceremony at Chapel Cemetery on September 21, 2024. *Courtesy Linda Hass.*

Sugar House Not So Sweet for Prisoners

During the late 1700s, raw sugar and molasses destined for refineries were stored in warehouses, usually multistory brick structures. Because these buildings, known as "sugar houses," had large storage capacity, many were used as prisons by occupying British forces during the American Revolutionary War. According to prisoners who survived, prison rations consisted of spoiled pork and soggy sea biscuits. The biscuits were often extremely moldy from sea water and infested with worms—a deplorable condition made consumable only by prisoners placing it in a kettle of water and skimming off the parasites.

Sally died in 1847, and on March 28, 1849, the ninety-year-old former ranger, militiaman and sailor took his last voyage. John Wall is buried beside his wife in Chapel Cemetery (see "Chapel Cemetery Honored"). Their sons Chester C. Wall (1807–1884) and Joseph Wall (1814–1849) also are buried there. Another relative may be Moses Wall (1807–1884), who also is buried in Chapel Cemetery. Their daughter Betsey (Wall) Allen (?–1865) is buried in South Center Eaton Cemetery, Charlotte, Eaton County.

According to a descendant quoted in a 1924 newspaper article, John and Sally were originally buried at the family's homestead on Territorial Road in Jackson County, then known as "Wall Farm." The descendant, Sarah Robson, continued: "John Wall [and] wife…were buried there and later were disinterred and placed in the Chapel cemetery (Sandstone Township)." This often happened when farmsteads were sold to new owners and the family wanted to safeguard the integrity of their ancestral burial sites. The article added that Wall Street in New York City was named for John Wall's brother William Wall. Several other descendants mentioned in the newspaper article were listed as living in Sandstone Township, which may explain why the bodies were moved to a cemetery there.

On September 21, 2024, the Lansing Chapter Daughters of the American Revolution dedicated a commemorative marker honoring John's service at Chapel Cemetery. The marker, placed between the headstones of John and his wife, Sally Wall, was sponsored by the Lansing chapter, with NSDAR approval. The dedication ceremony was attended by members of DAR and SAR, dignitaries and the public. "It is vitally important that we preserve history, promote patriotism, and honor those who fought for our nation at the time of its inception," said Brenda Nora of Jackson, a Lansing member and state co-chair of commemorative events for the DAR of Michigan. Wall's headstone is one of three Patriot grave markers in Chapel Cemetery. The other markers commemorate Samuel Hollister and Abiathar Lincoln, all mentioned in this book.

Like John, the Patriot described in the next chapter had very active and diverse tours of duty, from guarding forts to occupying a strategic hill during one of the most famous battles of the American Revolution.

Chapter 24

SWIFT WOODWORTH

Born to: Benjamin and Mercy (Swift) Woodworth on October 16, 1759
Birthplace: Lebanon, Connecticut
Moved to: Concord Township before 1836
Died: March 5, 1838
Burial: West Concord Cemetery, Concord Township

Patriot Swift Woodworth's first combat experience in the Revolutionary War was the Battle of Bunker Hill (June 17, 1775), a bloody confrontation that is highlighted in history books. The battle was prompted by British plans to occupy the high ground surrounding Boston, Massachusetts, in preparation for a siege. When colonial leaders learned of this plan, they ordered Patriot forces to get there first and deprive the British of this strategic advantage.

Swift, whose first name was his mother's maiden name, had no idea of these maneuverings when the sixteen-year-old first enlisted as a private in the Continental army in May 1775. All the Lebanon, Connecticut teenager knew was that he wanted to defend his homeland. His date with destiny was sealed, however, when his unit was assigned to march from Lebanon to Cambridge, Massachusetts, a distance of about 106 miles. Upon arrival, his unit received further instructions to march to nearby Boston and assist Patriot forces in stealthily occupying the hill. They did so on June 13, entrenching themselves in redoubts on Bunker Hill and Breed's Hill.

When the British suspected the Patriots had beaten them to the punch, they attacked on June 17 in an attempt to seize the tactical terrain. British troops ascended the hill in traditional battle formation. As they advanced, a Patriot officer worried about limited ammunition is said to have shouted, "Don't fire until you see the whites of their eyes!" Patriots waited until British troops neared the redoubt and then unleashed a deadly volley at almost point-blank range, decimating British lines and causing a hasty retreat among surviving British soldiers. One Patriot is said to have remarked afterward, "They advanced toward us in order to swallow us up, but they found a choaky [*sic*] mouthful of us."

British soldiers advanced up the hill a second time, stepping over the bodies of their dead comrades as they pushed forward, and once again they received a withering volley. Finally, on the third try, when Patriot forces had run out of ammunition, the British succeeded in breaking through the Patriot works. Casualties were high on both sides, but the surprising show of resistance by Patriots was a sobering demonstration of their determination and a wake-up call to British forces who had dismissed the opposition as a ragtag group of farmers and common people (see "The Battle of Bunker Hill").

One might think, after this baptism of fire, that Swift would not want to return to the fight. Instead, the plucky teen served several more tours from 1776 to 1780. His units' missions ranged from reinforcing Continental

The Battle of Bunker Hill, a painting by Howard Pyle (1847), illustrates typical British battle formation during the Revolutionary War. *Wikimedia Commons.*

Battle of Bunker Hill

The Battle of Bunker Hill (June 17, 1775) took place during the first stage of the Revolutionary War. The conflict is named after Bunker Hill, which, ironically, was only peripherally involved in the confrontation. The confrontation was prompted when Patriot forces learned that the British wanted to occupy the high ground in an attempt to surround Boston. Patriot forces decided to get there first and beat the enemy to the punch. They fought advancing enemy troops valiantly, ceding ground only after they ran out of ammunition. If the casualties and losses are any indication, the battle demonstrated beyond a doubt that an inexperienced militia was capable of standing up to regular army troops in battle. After the dust settled, about 1,054 British troops were killed or wounded, compared to only 405 Patriots.

troops to guarding forts. In addition, he labored as a teamster for six months in 1780 transporting continental provisions to General George Washington's army throughout New Jersey.

After the Revolution, Swift married a woman whose name has not yet been determined. The couple, who had at least one son, lived in Connecticut from 1783 to about 1831. In 1831, Swift moved to New York either with his wife or as a widower. One year later, the seventy-three-year-old Patriot filed for his pension. As part of the claim, a fellow Patriot who served with Swift at Fort Ticonderoga, New York, submitted a statement testifying to Swift's service. The claim was approved in 1833.

Sometime before 1836, Swift; his son, Charles; and Charles's wife, Desire (Babcock) Woodworth, felt the pull to head west, so the trio traveled to the Michigan Territory. Given that Swift's wife was not part of this move, it is likely she had died by this time. The family settled on farmland in what today is Concord Township.

Interestingly, when the township was officially named in 1837, the resident who chose the name was Thomas McGee, the son of another Revolutionary War Patriot who settled there—David McGee (also described in this book). Thomas said he was inspired to pick the name because of a spirit of concord, "peace and harmony" among residents. Perhaps that spirit of peace appealed to Swift, an elderly Patriot who had experienced various bloody battles.

This is the grave monument for Patriot Swift Woodworth, who is buried in West Concord Cemetery, Concord township. *Courtesy Linda Hass.*

In September 1836, Swift's daughter-in-law, Desire Woodworth, died and was buried on property Charles set aside as a family cemetery (today West Concord Cemetery, also known as Red Brick Cemetery, Concord Township). On March 5, 1838, at the age of seventy-eight, the Patriot whose introduction to the Revolutionary War was the Battle of Bunker

West Concord Cemetery, Concord Township, has the graves of Patriots from many wars, including Patriot Swift Woodworth. *Courtesy Linda Hass.*

Hill died. Although there are questions about his exact burial location in West Concord Cemetery, the authors believe he is indeed buried there for several reasons: his son, Charles, set aside land for the purpose of a family burial plot; Swift lived with Charles at the time of his (Swift's) death; Swift's headstone is there, although placed after his death; both Charles (1785–1852) and his wife, Desire Woodworth (1791–1836), are buried in the same cemetery; and Swift's grave site in that cemetery was also reviewed and approved by the Sarah Treat Prudden Chapter National Society Daughters of the American Revolution.

Today, the cemetery, which posts "no trespassing" signs, is on private property owned by Tricia Clark of Arizona. It is recommended that visitors wanting access to the property contact the Concord Township Board for information on how to contact Clark.

THIS BIOGRAPHY CONCLUDES THE last of the known Patriots who have credible evidence of their service in the Revolutionary War and who were connected to Jackson County. What can be gained from this exploration of Patriots' collective trials, tribulations and victories? This question was presented to a Jackson County focus group in which members represented different races, religions and ages and who had the opportunity to read the manuscript. None belonged to the DAR or SAR. This is a summary of their answers:

Most said that they developed a better understanding of Patriots' sacrifices and, as a result, a greater appreciation for liberties easily taken for granted. Some said the unity demonstrated by Patriots from different states, walks of life and ages—all fighting for a common cause—contributed to a feeling of national unity, since all Americans share the same national heritage. Educators and parents said the cemetery locator map and addresses for historic landmarks gave them ideas for potential school-related field trips. Some who recognized the surnames of Patriots said they were inspired to begin genealogical investigations. A few respondents wanted to know similar historical information about the counties that are contiguous to Jackson. While that topic is beyond the scope of this book, such exploration is certainly possible in the future. Finally, one respondent asked about proper cemetery visitation protocol.

Should readers be inspired to visit Patriots' graves, please be mindful of cemetery rules and regulations, which are usually posted on signs. Some cemeteries are located on private property, such as West Concord Cemetery, and require visitors to seek permission before entering. Other cemeteries with public access don't allow visitors to dig, use metal detectors or leave tangible objects (shrubs, etc.) without permission. Think of your visit as a time of respect for those who sacrificed much to secure the freedoms citizens enjoy today.

In addition to the Patriots described thus far, there are a few other potential Patriots whose evidence was questionable and, thus, didn't warrant a separate chapter. But they are mentioned in the next chapter on the chance that you, the reader, can provide more information about them. Read on to find out more about these mystery men.

Chapter 25

JACKSON'S MYSTERY PATRIOTS

In addition to the soldiers described previously, Jackson County has several "mystery Patriots" who might have served in the Revolutionary War but whose evidence trail presents more questions than answers. As a brief word of explanation on our eligibility standards, the Patriots featured in this book have credible evidence of service. They also are connected to Jackson County in one of three ways: they were either buried in, have grave monuments in or lived in the county. This standard differs from lineage-based organizations in that the Patriots mentioned in this book don't require a descendant to apply for membership in order to be recognized.

Also, our standard differs from the minimum six-month requirement set by the U.S. government for a pension because the authors count any time served as sufficient. So, for example, a Patriot may have served for weeks—not months; may not have a descendant; and may not even have a grave in Jackson County, but if there is credible evidence that he fought in the Revolution for any length of time, even as a substitute, and that he is connected to Jackson County, he is a candidate for inclusion.

What about the Patriots who lack definitive evidence? The answer is this chapter—an opportunity for them to be named collectively. This chapter also represents an opportunity for the authors to solicit help from you, the reader. Perhaps you have more information on these historical figures or on any of the Patriots described in this book? If so, please see Appendix A, "Request for Help," which has contact information.

Our first mystery Patriot is Samuel Graham Sr., whose mention in *Portrait and Biographical Album of Jackson County, Michigan* asserts that he served in the Revolutionary War and lived in Jackson County. An excerpt states: "Samuel Graham was a Scotsman by birth and emigrated to America in the latter part of the 1700s and in time to participate as a soldier in the Revolutionary War. He fought on the side of the Colonists and, when the struggle was ended, settled in the woods of Northern Ohio." It adds that he later left Ohio and "came to the wilds of Michigan and spent his last years in Parma Township, this county, dying when nearly ninety-six years old."

A Samuel Graham (1762–1840) is also listed by Find-A-Grave as a Patriot who died in 1840 at seventy-eight and was buried in Graham Cemetery, Parma Township. Find-A-Grave is a website that allows the public to add to an online database of cemetery records. One glaring inconsistency between Find-A-Grave and *Portrait and Biographical Album* is the almost twenty-year difference in the lifespans of their subjects (ninety-six versus seventy-eight years). A few years' difference could easily be dismissed, since ages and birth dates were often self-reported. Many early Americans did not know or could not accurately remember their birth years; thus, their descendants had to guess their age at death. Other times, census records were taken by those who misunderstood the information given or who made mistakes in documenting it. In still other cases, if language was a barrier or the resident was not home, census takers sometimes asked neighbors for facts like ages, leading to more guesses.

Even so, a variance of almost twenty years presents some obvious questions about whether the figures listed on Find-A-Grave and *Portrait and Biographical Album* are one and the same or two different individuals—perhaps father and son? Also, pension documents for a Patriot named Samuel Graham do not include any requests for transfers to Jackson County—or even Michigan for that matter. For these and other reasons, Samuel Graham is listed among our plausible Patriots requiring further research.

The next mystery Patriot is John Durand, who is categorized as "Not Established" with a lineage-based organization. According to the organization's registry, he was born in 1760 in Woodbury, Connecticut; died in 1852 in Jackson; and was buried in Mount Evergreen Cemetery. His birthdate is a mystery, however. According to the inscription on his grave monument, he died in 1852 at the age of eighty-two, which means he would have been born in 1770. If that is true, he would have been five years old when the Revolution began and only thirteen when it ended. Although there are several underage Patriots described in this book, this particular age range is especially questionable. The birth year listed in the lineage-based organization's registry—1760—reflects a more reasonable age for service, but it contradicts the date on his grave monument. So, for these and other reasons, John Durand is listed among our potential Patriots.

The next possible Patriot is B. Buirne, who also is categorized as "Not Established" with a lineage-based organization. According to the organization's registry, he was born in 1732 (birthplace unknown), died in 1811 in Michigan and was buried in Mount Evergreen Cemetery, Jackson. However, his residency and burial in Jackson are problematic for many reasons. First, Horace Blackman did not file a claim for property in what is now known as Jackson until 1829, and Mount Evergreen Cemetery was not established until 1843. These curious facts lead one to wonder how a person who died in 1811 could have lived in a village that was not founded for another eighteen years. Likewise, how could he have been buried in a cemetery that was not established until thirty-two years after his death? Also, in ongoing collaborations with the City of Jackson, which oversees the cemetery, his grave site could not be located. Additionally, there are no pension documents on his behalf to fill in details, since he died prior to any acts of the federal government providing for a pension. Given the numerous variations in the spelling of his surname (Burn, Born, Burne, Bourne, etc.) and the lack of a known first name, the mysterious "B. Buirne" is listed here.

The two remaining mystery Patriots are William Champe and someone identified as the father of Henry Lovewell. William Champe (1755–1834) is listed on Find-A-Grave as buried in Concord Township. The site's creator stated he served in the American Revolution; however, no military or other documents could be found to substantiate this claim. Also, his grave site in the cemetery could not be located, and there is no additional evidence to prove he lived in Jackson; thus, he is listed here as a "Mystery Patriot."

The father of Henry Lovewell (birth and death dates unknown; name unconfirmed) is mentioned in Find-A-Grave and in *Portrait and Biographical Album of Jackson County, Michigan* as a British soldier who defected and ended up fighting on the American side. However, there is no military or other evidence to substantiate this claim. It's also uncertain if Lovewell Sr. migrated with his son to Parma Township or if he remained in his native New York, since there is no evidence that he lived in Jackson. For these reasons, he is added to our "Mystery Patriot" section.

While mystery swirls around the Patriots mentioned in this chapter, Jackson is home to several unmistakable, tangible tokens of the Revolutionary War, not only in the form of grave monuments but also other touchable relics, including a 1,407-pound heavyweight that welcomes guests in a local museum. Read on to find out more about this centuries-old relic and one other.

PART III

JACKSON'S OTHER CONNECTIONS TO THE REVOLUTION

Chapter 26

A DRUM'S JOURNEY TO JACKSON

A drum that spurred Patriots of the American Revolution to rally against the British ended up in the attic of a Jackson home on Bush Street in the early 1900s, according to a *Jackson Citizen Patriot* newspaper article.

The resident who discovered the historical treasure, homeowner A.T. Curtis, was interviewed by the local paper in 1934. He told the reporter that when he ventured into the attic for the first time, the drum caught his attention because it showed construction techniques from earlier days. Curtis said that rats had destroyed much of the original leather and ropes, but the shell head and other parts of the frame endured, along with the sticks. Most interestingly, parts of the drum were held together with thirteen old, tarnished brass-headed tacks—a technique that he said was used during the Revolutionary War era to symbolize the thirteen original colonies.

This intriguing find inspired Curtis to research historic drums as well as the home's previous owner, a resident named Seymour Bates. Curtis discovered that Bates was the grandson of American Revolutionary War Patriot Francis Bates, who was born in the 1750s in Swansea, Massachusetts, and served in the Continental army during the American Revolution. The Bates patriarch, who was eighteen years old at the time of his service, is listed in the *Massachusetts U.S. Soldiers and Sailors in the Revolutionary War*, vol. 1, p. 787.

No evidence could be found confirming Bates's specific role as a drummer, but this role was not uncommon for teenagers at that time. Curtis was quoted as stating that he had researched the dark brown stains on the

PAGE EIGHT.

BLOODSTAINED DRUM

Was Found in Attic of Home Where Descendant of Drummer Boy Lived; Is Now in the Possession of A. T. Curtis.

A drum that spurred soldiers of the American Revolutionary war to do their best against the British in battle is the proud possession of A. T. Curtis, 840 Bush street, who has traced its history back to the days of the continental army.

Francis Bates, who carried the drum in battle, was born in the town of Swansey, Mass., in the 1750's.* At the age of 18, he was mustered into the Continental army as drummer boy by Muster Master James Leonard, Captain Drown's company, regiment commanded by Colonel Lee.

Son Gets Drum.

After the American patriots won their freedom and the war was brought to a close, Bates moved to

REVOLUTIONARY DRUM.

NAVY MAY ABANDON FORTIFICATIONS IN PHILIPPINE ISLANDS

Compromise Independence Arrangement Is Now Being Negotiated.

Washington, Feb. 24.—(AP)—The navy department is quietly studying a plan for abandonment of all military and naval fortifications and bases in the Philippines in event of independence for the islands.

The withdrawal would place Pearl Harbor in Hawaii as the naval spearhead in the Pacific, and would radically alter American operations in the Far East.

Naval Base On Island.

At present the navy maintains a major fortified naval base at Corregidor island, in the entrance to Manila bay, which is the headquarters for the Asiatic fleet.

In addition to this and other small naval stations, the government owns a dozen forts and army camps at which approximately 5,500 regular army troops and 6,000 Philippine scouts now are stationed. These are in various parts of the islands.

Under the terms of a compromise independence plan now being negotiated in Manila and Washington, United States would agree to surrender all military preserves in the islands when the Philippine republic was established.

Hawes Cutting Law.

Under the Hawes-Cutting law between 1946 and 1950, dependent upon the speed with which the Philippine constitution was written and other terms complied with.

Early developments toward Filipino acceptance of a compromise are anticipated as the result of cable exchanges with Manila this week. Manuel L. Quezon, president of the Philippine senate already has agreed to the plan in principle, and legislative leaders here are in contact now with opposition political leaders in Manila, seeking their cooperation.

conducted at Mount Union this week:

At Last! Angler's Y Of Lost Fish I

Grand Rapids, Mich.—William E. Camp is one fish does not have to endur of his pals when he the "big one that got a'

He has proof of his

Camp caught a bass guessed to weight a pounds, snapped him on chain stringer. But the denly jerked away while ered into the water, stringer with it.

Four days later Burt I other fisherman, saw a ently standing on its he surface of the water. H it up, found a chain st tached. He ate the fish, heard of Camp's story an the stringer.

The fish weighed nin pounds.

At The Th

Michigan.

Sunday, Monday, Tu Wednesday—William I "Fashions of 1934" Davis, Frank McHugh cast. On the stage, Spring Style Revue, wit and Sorita, "DeLuxe Da Michigan String Ensemb

Extra Tuesday evenin feature—James Cagney Brian in "Hard to Hand

Thursday, Friday and —Double feature bil Menjou and Genevieve "Easy to Love," with bee and Edward Evere and "Stan" Laurel ar Hardy in a feature com of the Desert" with Cha

The Michigan theater today, offers a combin and screen fare out of nary.

Jacobson's Spring St with living models will b ed for the first four da week and as a special traction "DeRosa and Deluxe Dancers, wh features of the Detroit club and the Congress F cago, will present thr numbers. The musical will be furnished by the String Ensemble, under

This February 25, 1934, *Jackson Citizen Patriot* article describes a Revolutionary War drum's journey to Jackson. *Courtesy Jackson District Library.*

drum's shell head and concluded they were from blood, hinting that Francis was wounded at one point. However the stains originated, there's no doubt that service during the Revolutionary War was a matter of blood, sweat and tears for many Revolutionary War soldiers who did not have the benefit of extensive medical care.

After the war, Bates moved to Buffalo, New York where his son Francis Bates Jr. was born. The newspaper article stated that in 1836, his son ventured to the Michigan Territory, traveling via ox team and bringing with him the treasured drum belonging to his Patriot father. Francis Jr. settled in Ovid, Branch County. At his death in the late 1800s, the drum was passed on to his son Seymour Bates, who apparently moved from Ovid to Jackson.

Over time, the drum that originally belonged to Seymour's grandfather found its way into the attic of his grandson's Jackson home, where it sat, neglected but quietly resonating with stories and experiences from the Revolutionary War. Its day of liberation arrived when new homeowner Curtis ventured into the dusty attic to take a look around. What should his wondering eyes behold, but the remnants of a historic treasure.

The relic prompted Curtis to launch an in-depth investigation into Revolutionary War drums and to restore this particular drum as historically accurately as possible. The authors' efforts to track down the drum's current fate or location have not been successful to date. Many possibilities exist, however, including its donation to a museum.

Regardless, the fact remains that at one time, this Revolutionary War relic came to Jackson. Fortunately, another authentic remnant of the Revolution not only remains in Jackson but is available for public viewing. Read on to find out more about this 1,407-pound treasure.

Chapter 27

A CANNON'S RESURRECTION

A cannon once meant to ward off American revolutionaries now greets American (and other) visitors almost as soon as they enter the Michigan Military Heritage Museum at 311 North Wisner Street in Jackson. The formidable piece of field artillery sits near the front door, weighing in at a whopping 1,407 pounds!

Accompanying it is a sign that describes the big gun's fascinating journey to its current post at the museum. Its long and winding travels included a voyage from England to Michigan, journeys on water and under it, use during the American Revolution and a final trip to Jackson—giving its host the distinction of being home to one of the oldest pieces of artillery in Michigan's military history.

The story behind the cannon's meanderings began with its birth in 1745. Like all weapons made in Great Britain at the time, its manufacture was controlled by the Board of Ordnance and was administered by a surveyor general who was responsible for ensuring standards were upheld governing the caliber, weight and length of all ordnance produced.

Jackson's cannon was among those that passed muster and was stamped with the crest of Great Britain's monarch at the time, King George II, who ruled from 1727 to 1760. Likely, neither the king nor the surveyor general had any idea that this particular cannon would be needed due to a revolution in one of Britain's upstart colonies—or that the cannon would end up in the permanent possession of that renegade nation.

Next, the big gun made a several-week voyage across the Atlantic by ship to North America around 1756. "It likely saw service on the East Coast in the French and Indian/Seven Years War (1756–1763), before being used in the British Merchant Fleet, since law required these ships to be armed," said Scott Gerych, chairman of the Michigan Military Heritage Museum. Generally, ships' masters were not too keen about this requirement, since the added weight meant ships could hold less merchandise, he added.

The next event in the life of this cannon was the American Revolution (1775–83), which prompted the British commander at Fort Detroit to request additional cannons be brought to the Michigan stronghold so it could control passage through the straits. British merchant sailors were only too happy to comply, and they eagerly gave up their heavy artillery, including the cannon that would end up in Jackson.

On a related note, it's amazing to consider that in 1776, when the New England colonies demanded independence from Great Britain, British rule in Detroit was unquestioned. In fact, Britain reinforced Fort Detroit with two hundred to three hundred additional soldiers in order to defend the post in case the Revolution spread westward. General George Washington even

This 1,407-pound British cannon, made in 1745 and used in the American Revolution, is displayed at the Michigan Military Heritage Museum in Jackson. *Courtesy Linda Hass.*

considered attacking Fort Detroit at one point, but he ultimately decided against it. Even so, the fort was used in the Revolution—to hold up to five hundred American prisoners. Perhaps this cannon was among armaments that contributed to a sense of intimidation among prisoners.

After the Revolutionary War ended and peaceful trade resumed between the United States and Britain, British soldiers got rid of the old cannons by taking them onto the frozen Detroit River and setting their wooden carriages on fire. The fires and steaming hot metal melted the ice, plunging the ordnance to the river bottom, where the submerged cannons lay hidden in the muck for over 190 years.

Then, in 1984, a curious diver with the Detroit Police Department saw mysterious objects in the murky depths and decided to take a closer look—and the rest, as they say, is history. This cannon and ten others were resurrected from the dark recesses of the river into the light of day, much to the delight of historians who marveled at the treasures.

This particular cannon ended up in the possession of the Detroit Historical Society (DHS), but it was not home yet. The field gun made its final voyage when the DHS long-term loaned it to the Michigan Military Heritage Museum (MMHM) in Jackson, which, in turn, had the gun and carriage restored by Mike Coppernoll of Grass Lake, with MMHM assistance.

Today, the former weapon of war has been resurrected as an object of welcome and curiosity at the museum. And it has the distinction of being one of the few authentic Revolutionary War artifacts that Jacksonians can behold—and touch—in their own hometown.

Appendix A

REQUEST FOR HELP

The authors have done their best to visit the graves of the Revolutionary War soldiers buried in Jackson County, examining eighteen known graves out of the twenty-two Patriots mentioned in this book. We have consulted pension statements, burial and cemetery records and much more. But there is one source that we have not been able to access until now—you, the reader! We call on our readers, local genealogists and those with personal knowledge of these veterans to help us fill in the blanks.

If you have additional information about the Patriots highlighted in this book, including where graves are located, or if you know of any additional Revolutionary War Patriots not mentioned in this book who are buried in Jackson County, please contact coauthor David Van Hoof at david.w.vanhoof@gmail.com. Thank you.

Appendix B

RESOURCES

Hopefully this book has helped to make the Revolutionary War personal for Jackson residents by highlighting the Patriots connected to Jackson County. These Patriots represent the tip of the iceberg on this expansive topic. If you would like to learn more about the American Revolution (1775–83), following is a brief sampling of pertinent local and state museums, libraries, organizations and resources:

Jackson County

A Virtual Cemetery Created by Deb Hayes Wolfe at www.findagrave.com/virtual-cemetery/176672?page=1#sr-14918360

Jackson County Michigan Historical Society
P.O. Box 1856
Jackson, MI 49204
www.myjacksonhistorical.org
Coauthor Linda Hass is a member of this society.

Jackson County Genealogical Society
211 West Ganson Street, Suite 170
Jackson County, MI 49204
517-768-9266
jcgsmi.org

This nonprofit volunteer organization maintains a library and is dedicated to local genealogy. Coauthor David Van Hoof is a member of this society.

Jackson District Library
Serves all of Jackson County through thirteen community libraries and through its "virtual" branch at this website: myjdl.com/about/about
Following is contact information for the main branch:

Carnegie Library
244 West Michigan Avenue
Jackson, MI 49203
517-788-4087
The reference desk on the main floor may be a helpful first stop.

Michigan Military Heritage Museum
311 North Wisner Street
Jackson, MI 49202
517-926-6696
mimhm.org
This museum has a small collection of Revolutionary War artifacts.

Michigan and Beyond
Two nonprofit service organizations that revolve around the American Revolution are the *National Society Daughters of the American Revolution* (NSDAR) and the *National Society Sons of the American Revolution* (NSSAR). For more information on the NSDAR, which has a Jackson Chapter called the Sarah Treat Prudden Chapter, contact Sarahtreatpruddenchapternsdar@gmail.com. The Sarah Treat Prudden Chapter has marked several of the graves mentioned in this book. For more information on the NSSAR, which does not have a chapter in Jackson but has several chapters throughout Michigan, see missar.org. This organization, of which coauthor David Van Hoof is a member, also has marked several graves mentioned in this book. The authors are indebted to both these worthwhile organizations for their contributions to this subject matter.

Fort Michilimackinac State Park
102 Straits Avenue
Mackinaw City, MI 49701

906-847-3328
This state park includes historic Fort Michilimackinac (est. 1779). For more information, see www.mackinacparks.com/explore.

University of Michigan William L. Clements Library
This library provides online access to its Revolutionary War manuscript collection.

909 South University Avenue
Ann Arbor, MI 48109
734-764-2347
clements.umich.edu/u-m-clements-library-announces-online-access-to-popular-revolutionary-war-manuscript-collection

Appendix C

PATRIOT CEMETERY MAP

This map shows approximately where Patriots are buried in Jackson County. Patriots whose exact burial sites are unknown have an asterisk beside their name, indicating that they are represented by the township hall of the township in which they lived during their last days.

Cemetery Locator for American Revolutionary War Patriots

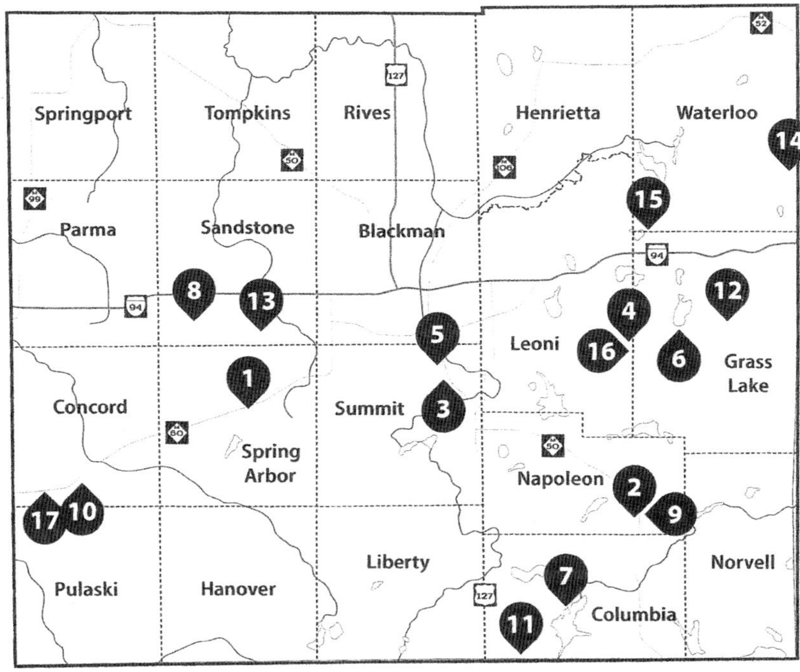

Jackson County Patriot Cemetery Guide

1 **Lemuel Benedict:** Spring Arbor Cemetery, 340 E. Main St., Spring Arbor

2 ***Sylvanus Blackman:** 6755 Brooklyn Rd., Napoleon

3 **Joseph Darling: Woodland Cemetery,** 2615 Francis St., Summit

4 ***Joseph Efner:** 913 Fifth St., Michigan Center, Leoni

5 **John Gibson, Jabez Mosher, Jonathan Thompson:** Mt. Evergreen Cemetery, 1047 Greenwood Ave., **City of Jackson**

6 ***Rhodes Hall:** 373 Lakeside Dr., Grass Lake

7 **David Haynes:** Jefferson Cemetery, Hewitt Rd., Columbia

8 **Samuel Hollister, Abiathar Lincoln, John Wall:** Chapel Cemetery, E. Michigan Ave., Sandstone

9 **Daniel Jones:** unknown grave, Oak Grove Cemetery, Brooklyn Rd., Napoleon

10 **David McGee:** Maple Grove Cemetery, Main & 3rd Streets, Concord

11 **Abraham Osborn, Thomas Swartout:** Cement City Cemetery, Cary Rd., Columbia

12 **Adam Overacker:** Grass Lake East Cemetery, E. Michigan Ave, Grass Lake

13 **John Perrin(e):** Dearing Cemetery, E. Michigan Ave., Sandstone

14 **Isaac Quigley:** Mt. Hope Cemetery, Loveland Rd., Waterloo

15 **Daniel Thurston:** Mt. Pleasant Cemetery, Seymour Rd., Waterloo

16 **Samuel Underwood:** Leoni Township Cemetery, 184 S. Portage Rd., Leoni

17 **Swift Woodworth:** West Concord Cemetery, M-60/Homer Rd., Concord

**Asterisk indicates township address since exact grave site in township is unknown*

BIBLIOGRAPHY

Introduction

American Revolution Institute. "Why the American Revolution Matters." https://www.americanrevolutioninstitute.org/why-the-american-revolution-matters.

Naseem, Saba. "How Much History Do Americans Actually Know? Less Than You Think." *Smithsonian Magazine*, May 28, 2015. www.smithsonianmag.com/history/how-much-us-history-do-americans-actually-know-less-you-think-180955431.

Warren, Jack D. "Why Is the American Revolution So Important?" American Heritage, Spring 2024. www.americanheritage.com/why-american-revolution-so-important.

Chapter 1

Deming, Brian. *Jackson: An Illustrated History.* Windsor Publications, 1984, 11–41.

Encyclopedia Britannica. "Erie Canal." www.britannica.com/topic/Erie-Canal.

Find-A-Grave. "Dr. Huldah Cotton Darling." www.findagrave.com/memorial/24221489/huldah-darling.

Hass, Linda. *The Hidden History of Jackson County, Michigan.* The History Press, 2020, 66, 144–45.

———. *Michigan's Crossroads to Freedom: The Underground Railroad in Jackson County.* St. Booklocker, 2017, 29–36.

History. "Congress Enacts the Northwest Ordinance." www.history.com/this-day-in-history/congress-enacts-the-northwest-ordinance.

———. "Proclamation of 1763." www.history.com/topics/native-american-history/1763-proclamation-of.

Littell, McDougal. *The Americans.* Evanston, IL, 2008, 39–76.

National Archives and Records Administration Bounty warranties. "Bounty Land Warranties for Military Service, 1775–1855." www.archives.gov.

Portrait and Biographical Album of Jackson County, Michigan, Containing Full Page Portraits and Biographical Sketches, Portraits & Biographies of All the Governors of the State and of the Presidents of the United States. Chapman Brothers, 1890, 812–13.

The McGee property, located in section 22 of Concord Township, also is represented on period maps.

Chapter 2

Wyatt, Ken. "Peek Through Time: Charting Jackson's Rise and Fall in Population." *Jackson Citizen Patriot*, September 30, 2013. www.mlive.com/news/jackson/2015/09/peek_through_time_charting_jac.html.

———. "Peek Through Time: St. Joseph Trail Played an Important Part in the Settlement of Jackson." *Jackson Citizen Patriot*, October 23, 2010. www.mlive.com/living/jackson/2010/10/peek_through_time_st_joseph_tr.html.

Chapter 3

DAR Application 9967, Elizabeth R. MacCarthy, 344–45, vol. 10, Lineage Book of the DAR Charter Members, great-granddaughter of Lemuel and Annis; DAR Application 14161, Sarah Benedict Saunder, 60, vol. 15, Lineage Book of the DAR Charter Members, granddaughter of E. Lemuel Benedict and Annis; mother of Elizabeth R. MacCarthy.

DeLand, Charles. *DeLand's History of Jackson County, Michigan.* B.F. Bowen Publisher, 1903, 101, 149, 254, 313.

Encyclopedia.com. "Continental Army." www.encyclopedia.com/history/encyclopedias-almanacs-transcripts-and-maps/continental-army-draft.

Find-A-Grave. "Abigail Hannah Benedict Riggs (1778–1860)," created by Elijah Shalis. www.findagrave.com/memorial/173337349/abigail_hannah_riggs.

———. "Annis Hitchcock Benedict." www.findagrave.com/memorial/261155306/annis_benedict.

———. "E. Lemuel Benedict (1764–1839)," created by Frank Passic. www.findagrave.com/memorial/15114967/e-lemuel-benedict

———. "Mary Benedict Morris (1768–1852)," created by Miss BeeHavin. www.findagrave.com/memorial/8906929/mary_morris.

———. "Moses Benedict (1796–1865)," created by Wilton Golson. www.findagrave.com/memorial/26791865/moses-benedict.

———. "Phoebe Benedict Pringle (1776–1861)," created by CW. www.findagrave.com/memorial/59608833/phoebe_benedict.

Hatcher, Patricia Law. *Abstract of Graves of Revolutionary Patriots.* Vol. 1. Pioneer Heritage Press, 1987, 25.

Jackson Citizen Patriot. "Early Days Are Recalled in Genealogical Records Read on Memorial Day." June 5, 1923.

Jonathan Benedict (Sgt, Cpt Hicok's Co., Col Elmore's Rgt., NY Line, American Revolution), pension no. W. 23579. *Case Files of Pension and Bounty-Land; Warrant Applications Based on Revolutionary War Service, compiled ca. 1800–ca. 1912, documenting the period ca. 1775–ca. 1900*; Record Group 15; National Archives, Washington, D.C.

Lemuel Benedict's service is "presumed" with the Sons of the American Revolution (SAR). He is listed in the registry of the DAR, but future DAR applicants must prove correct service. Other sources list Benedict's birth year as 1767; however, his headstone, which is from the period when he died, states he died at the age of seventy-five in 1839, which would make his birth year 1764.

Chapter 4

Arnold, James N. *Vital Records of Rhode Island 1636–1850.* Vol. 3, *Providence County.* Narragansett Historical Publishing Company, 1892, 46.

Burton, Clarence. *Governors and Judges Journal: Proceedings of the Land Board of Detroit.* Detroit, MI, 1915, 222.

Prologue Magazine. "Using Revolutionary War Pension Files to Find Family Information." www.archives.gov/publications/prologue/2015/summer/rev-war-pensions.html.

Sylvanus Blackman/Blackmar (Pvt., Cpt Windsor's Co., Col Brown's Rgt., Rhode Island Militia), pension no. R. 900. *Case Files of Pension and Bounty-Land; Warrant Applications Based on Revolutionary War Service, compiled ca. 1800–ca. 1912, documenting the period ca. 1775–ca. 1900.* Record Group 15; National Archives, Washington, D.C.

Travel Through Time. "Woodward Avenue: The Backbone of Detroit." historynavigator.org/2019/08/18/woodward-avenue-the-backbone-of-detroit.

U.S. Census, 1840.

Sylvanus Blackman is listed in the SAR registry based on his service pension application; he is not listed in the DAR registry.

Chapter 5

Find-A-Grave. "Huldah Darling (1764–1841)," created by Deb Hayes-Wolfe. www.findagrave.com/memorial/24221489/huldah-darling.

———. "Joseph Darling (1764–1844)," created by Deb Hayes-Wolfe. www.findagrave.com/memorial/24210553/joseph-darling.

History Net. "Then and Now: The Great Chain of West Point, N.Y." www.historynet.com/west-point-chain.

Joseph Darling (Pvt., Cpt. Wilder's Co., Col. Neslon's Rgt., Mass. Militia, American Revolution), pension no. S. 29110. *Case Files of Pension and Bounty-Land; Warrant Applications Based on Revolutionary War Service, compiled ca. 1800–ca. 1912, documenting the period ca. 1775–ca. 1900.* Record Group 15; National Archives, Washington, D.C. Joseph Darling is listed in the DAR registry. Although no descendant has applied for membership in the SAR, that organization recognizes/accepts his service.

National Library of Medicine. "Decennial Life Tables for the White Population of the United States, 1790–1900." pmc.ncbi.nlm.nih.gov/articles/PMC2885717.

Portrait & Biographical Album of Jackson, Michigan. Chapman Bros. Pub., 1890, 324.

Wyatt, Ken. "Peek Through Time: More Than Beautiful Acreage behind the Namesake of Loomis Park." *Jackson Citizen Patriot*, March 30, 2016. www.mlive.com/news/jackson/2016/03/peek_through_time_more_than_be.html.

One other source lists Darling's year of death as 1841. The Patriot's pension statement suggests a date of 1844, which is the date used for this biography.

Other Darling children buried in Michigan are Mary C. "Polly" (Darling) David (1798–1868, buried in Chamberlin Cemetery, Van Buren County); Christopher C. Darling (1800–1880, buried in Mount Hope Cemetery, Ingham County); and Pascal P. Darling (1802–1846, buried in Rosehill Cemetery, Eaton Rapids).

Chapter 6

Find-A-Grave. "Joseph Efner (1759–1843)," created by Sunshine. www.findagrave.com/memorial/16706015/joseph-efner.

———. "Ruth Efner (1759–1798)," created by Sunshine. www.findagrave.com/memorial/16705869/ruth-efner.

Hudson Valley. "Fanning the Flames." hvmag.com/life-style/fanning-the-flames.

Joseph Efner/Efnor (Pvt., Cpt. Lansing's Co., Col. Wemple's Rgt., NY Militia), pension no. S. 29777. *Case Files of Pension and Bounty-Land; Warrant Applications Based on Revolutionary War Service, compiled ca. 1800–ca. 1912, documenting the period ca. 1775–ca. 1900.* Record Group 15; National Archives, Washington, D.C.

Office of the State Comptroller. *New York in the Revolution.* Albany, NY: J.B. Lyon & Co., 1904, 101.

Joseph Efner is listed in the SAR registry; he is not listed in the DAR registry.

Chapter 7

Amos Perkins (Sgt., Capt. Gibbs' Co., Col. Richmond's Regiment, Rhode Island Line), pension no. W. 16369. *Case Files of Pension and Bounty-Land; Warrant Applications Based on Revolutionary War Service, compiled ca. 1800–ca. 1912, documenting the period ca. 1775–ca. 1900.* Record Group 15; National Archives, Washington, D.C.

Deming, Brian. Jackson: An Illustrated History. Windsor Publications, 1984, 12–16.

Find-A-Grave. "Amasa B. Gibson (1795–1868)," created by Deb Hayes-Wolfe. www.findagrave.com/memorial/57748389/amasa-b-gibson.

———. "Mary Hay Douglass Gibson (1800–1852)," created by Frank Passic. www.findagrave.com/memorial/16893071/mary-hay-gibson.

John Gibson (Pvt., Capt. Gibbs' Co., Col. Richmond's Rgt, Rhode Island Line), pension no. S. 34899. *Case Files of Pension and Bounty-Land; Warrant Applications Based on Revolutionary War Service, compiled ca. 1800–ca. 1912, documenting the period ca. 1775–ca. 1900.* Record Group 15; National Archives, Washington, D.C.

Lewis, Helen F. *Southeastern Michigan Pioneer Families: Especially Jackson County and New York Origins.* Rhinebeck, NY, 1998, 157.

Membership Application. James Gibson Jr., National no. 14478, John Gibson (1747–1848, Rhode Island), approved November 6, 1901. National Society Sons of the American Revolution, Officer of the Registrar General, Louisville, KY.

Membership Application. Mabel Gibson, National no. 42450, on John Gibson (1747–1848, Rhode Island), approved December 31, 1902. National Daughters of the American Revolution, Office of the Registrar General, Washington, D.C.

Walker, Anthony. *So Few the Brave.* Rhode Island Society of the Sons of the American Revolution, 1981, 122.

William Richardson (Pvt., Capt. Gibbs' Co., Col. Richmond's Regiment, Rhode Island Line), pension no. W. 16696. *Case Files of Pension and Bounty-Land; Warrant Applications Based on Revolutionary War Service, compiled ca. 1800–ca. 1912, documenting the period ca. 1775–ca. 1900.* Record Group 15; National Archives, Washington, D.C.

John Gibson's service is "presumed" by the SAR, based on his pension and other documents. He is not listed in the DAR registry.

Chapter 8

American Battlefield Trust. "Black Valor at Princeton." www.battlefields.org/learn/articles/black-valor-princeton.

Arnold, James. *Vital Records of Rhode Island 1626–1850.* 1st Series, Vol. 5, Part II: *South Kingston.* Narragansett Historical Publishing Company, 1894, 106.

1840 U.S. Census Springport Twp., Jackson County, M, HH—James Henderson, 182.

History. "Benedict Arnold Orders Burning of New London." www.history.com/this-day-in-history/arnold-orders-burning-of-new-london.

Ledgers of Payments, 1818–1872, to U.S. Pensioners Under Acts of 1818 Through 1858 from Records of the Office of the Third Auditor of the Treasury. Microfilm publication T718, 23 rolls. *Records of the Accounting Officers of the Department of the Treasury, 1775–1978*, Record Group 217. National Archives, Washington, D.C. 1840 (Michigan Territory—Jackson County).

Rhodes Hall (Mariner & Pvt., Cpt. Thompson's Co., Col. Lippett's Rgt., RI Line, Continental Army, American Revolution), pension no. S. 29206. *Case Files of Pension and Bounty-Land; Warrant Applications Based on Revolutionary War Service, Compiled ca. 1800–ca. 1912, Documenting the Period ca. 1775–ca. 1900.* Record Group 15; National Archives, Washington, D.C.

Rhodes Hall's service is "presumed" by the SAR, due to his pension application. He is not listed in the DAR registry.

Chapter 9

American Battlefield Trust. "The Fighting Man of the Continental Army." www.battlefields.org/learn/articles/fighting-man-continental-army.

The American Revolution Institute. "A Revolution in Arms: Weapons in the War for Independence." www.americanfirearms.org/weapons-firearms-american-revolution.

David Haynes (Pvt., Cpt. Bradley's Co., Col. Ross' Rgt., PA Militia, American Revolution), pension no. S. 8652. *Case Files of Pension and Bounty-Land; Warrant Applications Based on Revolutionary War Service, Compiled ca. 1800–ca. 1912, Documenting the Period ca. 1775–ca. 1900.* Record Group 15; National Archives, Washington, D.C.

Find-A-Grave. "David Haynes (1762–1844)," created by Debi Hayes-Wolfe. www.findagrave.com/memorial/18874189/david-haynes.

———. "James Enoch Haynes (1813–1868)," created by Debi Hayes-Wolfe. www.findagrave.com/memorial/17641609/james-enoch-haynes.

———. "Margaret Haynes (1775–1836)," created by Butterfly-kisses. www.findagrave.com/memorial/74989939/margaret-haynes.

David Haynes is listed in the DAR registry. Although no descendant has applied for membership in the SAR, that organization recognizes/accepts his service.

Other Haynes children buried in Michigan are Mary Ann (Haynes) Harrison (1792–1844, buried Union Chapel Cemetery, Wayne County) and Hannah (Haynes) Matthews (1804–1848, buried Dutch Settlement Cemetery, Branch County).

Chapter 10

"The American Revolution: An Everyday Life Perspective." maass.nyu.edu/resources/r1/lesson_plans/health.html.

Find-A-Grave. "Betsey Hollister (1766–1855)," created by Nadeen Sobotka. www.findagrave.com/memorial/80460520/betsey-hollister.

———. "Henry S. Hollister (1799–1861)," created by Frank Passic._www.findagrave.com/memorial/14546141/henruy-s-hollister.

———. "Samuel Hollister (1764–1842)," created by Debra Hayes-Wolfe. www.findagrave.com/memorial/19457934/samuel-hollister.

———. "Smith Hollister (1762–1851)," created by wienerin. www.findagrave.com/memorial/84891536/smith-hollister.

Lewis, Helen F. *Southeastern Michigan Pioneer Families: Especially Jackson County and New York Origins.* Kinship, 1998, 201–2.

Office of the State Comptroller. *New York in the Revolution.* J.B. Lyon & Co., 1904, 80.

Secretary of the Commonwealth. *Massachusetts Soldiers & Sailors of the American Revolution.* Vol. 8. Wright & Potter Printing Co., 1901, 146.

Smith Hollister (Pvt., Cpt. Quigley's Co., Col. Mitchell's Rgt., NJ Militia, American Revolution), pension no. S. 13461. *Case Files of Pension and Bounty-Land; Warrant Applications Based on Revolutionary War Service, Compiled ca. 1800–ca. 1912, Documenting the Period ca. 1775–ca. 1900.* Record Group 15; National Archives, Washington, D.C

Wallace Case, Lafayette. *The Hollister Family in America.* Fergus Printing Co., 1886, 81–82.

Samuel Hollister is listed in the DAR registry. Although no descendant has applied for membership in the SAR, that organization recognizes/accepts his service.

Chapter 11

DeLand, Charles. *DeLand's History of Jackson County, Michigan.* B.F. Bowen Publisher, 1903, 342–43.

Find-A-Grave. "Bethany Pierce Jones (1761–1847)," created by Christine Smith. www.findagrave.com/memorial/261412206/bethany-jones.

———. "Daniel Jones (1756–1847)," created by Deb Hayes-Wolfe. www.findagrave.com/memorial/107790185/daniel-jones.

———. "Joshua Jones (1787–1868)," created by Deb Hayes-Wolfe. www.findagrave.com/memorial/19919105/joshua-jones.

———. "Thankful Jones (1792–1868)," created by Deb Hayes-Wolfe. www.findagrave.com/memorial/19919114/thankful-jones.

National Museum of American History. "You Asked, We Answered: What Did Soldiers Eat During the Revolutionary War?" americanhistory.si.edu/explore/stories/you-asked-we-answered-what-did-soldiers-eat-during-revolutionary-war.

Secretary of the Commonwealth. *Massachusetts Soldiers & Sailors of the American Revolution.* Vol. 8. Wright & Potter Printing Co., 1901, 905.

State of Massachusetts. *Massachusetts, U.S., Compiled Birth, Marriage, and Death Records, 1700–1850.* Village of Dighton.

———. *Massachusetts, U.S., Town & Vital Records, 1620–1988.* Village of Dighton.

Daniel Jones died on April 14, 1847, per Kelly L. VanWormer and Pamela Hotary, "America 250: Daughters of the American Revolution: Revolutionary War Soldiers Buried in Michigan," booklet, DAR.

Daniel Jones is listed in the DAR and SAR registries.

Chapter 12

Abiathar/Abierther Lincoln Osborn (Pvt., Cpt. Thayer's Co., Col. Marshall's Rgt., Mass. Militia, American Revolution), pension no. S. 29296. *Case Files of Pension and Bounty-Land; Warrant Applications Based on Revolutionary War Service, Compiled ca. 1800–ca. 1912, documenting the period ca. 1775–ca. 1900.* Record Group 15; National Archives, Washington, D.C.

American Battlefield Trust. "Revolutionary War Strategy: What Causes/Effects for Both Sides Aided or Prevented Victory in the War?" www.battlefields.org/learn/articles/revolutionary-war-strategy.

Find-A-Grave. "Abiathar Lincoln (1759–1844)," created by Frank Passic. www.findagrave.com/memorial/14614724/abiathar-lincoln.

———. "Anna Lincoln Wood (1792–1857)," created by Judith Pierce Gunnett. www.findagrave.com/memorial/42130168/anna-wood.

———. "Jotham Wood (1786–1862)," created by Frank Passic. www.findagrave.com/memorial/14932021jotham-wood.

———. "Mary Babbitt Lincoln (1767–1837)," created by Frank Passic. www.findagrave.com/memorial/14614714/mary-lincoln.

Silliman, Sue Imogene. *Michigan Military Records: The D.A.R. of Michigan Historical Collections: Records of the Revolutionary Soldiers Buried in Michigan; The Pensioners of Territorial Michigan; and the Soldiers of Michigan Awarded the "Medal of Honor."* Michigan Historical Commission, 1920, 55.

We Are THE MIGHTY Military News. "Why Armies Used to Fight in Long Lines While Marching in the Open." www.wearethemighty.com/mighty-history/why-armies-used-to-fight-in-long-lines-while-marching-in-the-open.

Abiathar Lincoln is listed in the DAR and SAR registries.

Chapter 13

Belcher, Denis. "DAR to Designate Grave at Concord." *Jackson Citizen Patriot*, July 2, 1967.

Daniel McGee (Pvt., Cpt. Densmore's Co., Col. Woodbridge's Rgt., Mass. Militia, American Revolution), pension no. R. 6716. *Case Files of Pension and Bounty-Land; Warrant Applications Based on Revolutionary War Service, Compiled ca. 1800–ca. 1912, Documenting the Period ca. 1775–ca. 1900.* Record Group 15; National Archives, Washington, D.C.

Find-A-Grave. "David McGee (1760–1852)," created by Frank Passic. www.findagrave.com/memorial/13816750/david-mcgee.

———. "Mary Kendall McGee (1768–1853)," created by Frank Passic. www.findagrave.com/memorial/13816754/mary-mcgee.

———. "Thomas McGee (1790–1869)," created by Deb Hayes-Wolfe. www.findagrave.com/memorial/13816741/thomas-mcgee.

Maloy, Mark. "'The Hard Winter' of 1779–1780." Emerging Revolutionary War Era. emergingrevolutionarywar.org/2016/01/23/the-hard-winter-of-1779-1780.

David McGee's service is "presumed" with the SAR. He is registered with the DAR, but his listing is considered "NE/Not Established" because no person has joined the DAR through his lineage.

Melville's quote is taken from numerous documents, including *Michigan's Crossroads to Freedom*, published by Linda Hass (Booklocker.com, 2017), 32.

Chapter 14

American Citizen. "Deaths." November 19, 1951, 3.

Find-A-Grave. "Abagail Deake Mosher (1765–1828)," created by Phyllis Meyer. www.findagrave.com/memorial/43473631/abagail-mosher.

———. "Benjamin Mosher (1809–1874)," created by Susan Baker. www.findagrave.com/memorial/17978531/benjamin_gool_mosher.

———. "Hezekiah Mosher (1756–1821)," created by Julie (Gassman) Brewster. www.findagrave.com/memorial/108645074/hezekiah-mosher.

———. "Jabez Mosher Jr. (1759–1851)," created by Deb Hayes-Wolfe. www.findagrave.com/memorial/16952919/jabez-mosher.

———. "Mariah Mosher (1762–1842; birth & death years incorrect; birth year most likely 1784/85; death date August 17, 1863, per widow's pension)," created by Phyllis Meyer. www.findagrave.com/memorial/43473676/mariah-mosher.

Hidden New Jersey. "America's First Cattle Drive? Salem County's Great Cow Chase." www.hiddennj.com/2015/07/americas-first-cattle-drive-salem.html#:~:text=Washington%20sent%20Wayne%20with%20about%20550%20troops%20down,where%20they%20gathered%20about%20150%20head%20of%20cattle.

Jabez Mosher Jr. (Pvt., Cpt. Mosher's Co., Col. Van Woert's Rgt., NY Militia, American Revolution), pension no. W. 5392. *Case Files of Pension and Bounty-Land; Warrant Applications Based on Revolutionary War Service, Compiled ca. 1800–ca. 1912, documenting the period ca. 1775–ca. 1900*. Record Group 15; National Archives, Washington, D.C.

Office of the State Comptroller. *New York in the Revolution*. J.B. Lyon & Co., 1904, 131, 237.

Jabez Mosher's service is listed in the DAR registry. Although no descendant has applied for membership in the SAR, that organization recognizes/accepts his service.

Chapter 15

Abraham Osborn (Pvt., Cpt. Wisner's Co., Col. Hathorn's Rgt., NY Militia, American Revolution), pension no. S. 29356. *Case Files of Pension and Bounty-Land; Warrant Applications Based on Revolutionary War Service, Compiled ca. 1800–ca. 1912, Documenting the Period ca. 1775–ca. 1900.* Record Group 15; National Archives, Washington, D.C.

(Adrian) *Daily Telegram.* "Cement City." May 5, 1926.

———. "Cement City." May 19, 1926.

Find-A-Grave. "Abraham Osborn (1755–1843)," created by Deb Hayes-Wolfe. www.findagrave.com/memorial/21562024/abraham-osborn.

———. "Loretta Osborn (1762–1841)," created by Deb Hayes-Wolfe. www.findagrave.com/memorial/21561863/loretta-osborn.

———. "Samuel Finch (1757–1839)," created by Cole. www.findagrave.com/memorial/87400731/samuel-finch.

Kalamazoo Gazette. "Will Unveil Monument to Soldier of 1776." May 22, 1926.

"Revolutionary Soldier and His Wife Honored: Monuments Unveiled and Exercises at Cement City Cemetery." Undated newspaper clip posted in ancestry.com.

Samuel Finch (Pvt., Cpt. Sawyer's Co., Col. McLaughry's Rgt., NY Militia, American Revolution), pension no. R. 3543. *Case Files of Pension and Bounty-Land; Warrant Applications Based on Revolutionary War Service, Compiled ca. 1800–ca. 1912, documenting the period ca. 1775–ca. 1900.* Record Group 15; National Archives, Washington, D.C.

Abraham Osborn's service is listed in the DAR registry. Although no descendant has applied for membership in the SAR, that organization recognizes/accepts his service.

In Osborn's federal pension file, the government uses both 1841 and 1843 as the year of death in their communications, as well as stating "unknown"; hence, both dates are given for this biography.

Chapter 16

Adam Overacker/Overocker (Pvt., Cpt. Pecks's Co., Col. Yates' Rgt., New York Line, American Revolution), pension no. W. 2399. *Case Files of Pension and Bounty-Land; Warrant Applications Based on Revolutionary War Service, Compiled ca. 1800–ca. 1912, Documenting the Period ca. 1775–ca. 1900.* Record Group 15; National Archives, Washington, D.C.

1840 U.S. census listing. "Adam Overocker" in Grass Lake.

Find-A-Grave. "Adam Overacker (1761–1842)," created by Lynnsdaughter. www.findagrave.com/memorial/10469376/adam-overacker.

———. "Catherine Overacker Francisco (1796–1851)," created by Lynnsdaughter. www.findagrave.com/memorial/10476101/catherine-francisco.

———. "Michael Anthony Overacker (1785–1833)," created by Lynnsdaughter. www.findagrave.com/memorial/15695615/michael_anthony_overacker.

Silliman, Sue Imogene. *Michigan Military Records: The DAR of Michigan Historical Collections: Records of the Revolutionary Soldiers Buried in Michigan, the Pensioners of Territorial Michigan and the Soldiers of Michigan Awarded the "Medal of Honor."* Michigan Historical Commission, 1920, 129.

Adam Overacker's service is listed in the DAR and SAR registries.

The only other Overacker child to be buried in Michigan is Michael Anthony (1785–1833, bur. Felt Plains Cemetery, Ingham County). See above referenced Find-A-Grave citation for Michael Anthony Overacker.

While Overacker was born in Beekman Precinct, New York, his pension states he was a resident of Schaghticoke, New York, when he enlisted.

Chapter 17

Find-A-Grave. "Catherine Williamson Perrine (1759–1792)," created by Anne Mount West. www.findagrave.com/memorial/22562198/catherine-perrine.

———. "Henry Perrine (1786–1853)," created by Frank Passic. www.findagrave.com/memorial/10394975/henry-perrine.

———. "John Perrine (1760–1831)," created by Frank Passic. www.findagrave.com/memorial/10394957/john-perrine.

History. "Whiskey Rebellion." www.history.com/topics/early-us/whiskey-rebellion.

Perrine, Howland Delano. *Daniel Perrine "the Huguenot" and His Descendants in America, of the Surnames Perrine, Perine, and Prine, 1665–1910*. Press of Tobias A. Wright, 1910, 60–62, 107–8, 200–01.

Perrine, John. *U.S. Compiled Service Records of Soldiers Who Served in the American Army During the Revolutionary War, 1775–1783*. Monmouth County Militia, NJ, n.d.

Roos, David. "How the Erie Canal Was Built with Raw Labor and Amateur Engineering." History. www.history.com/news/erie-canal-construction-engineering-labor.

John Perrine is registered with the SAR. He is listed in the DAR registry but is considered "Not Established" because no person has joined the DAR through his lineage.

The only other Perrine child to be buried in Michigan is Catherine (Perrine) Bullard (1795–1876, bur. Mt. Rest Cemetery, Clinton County).

Chapter 18

American Battlefield Trust. "Monmouth (Monmouth Courthouse)." www.battlefields.org/learn/revolutionary-war/battles/monmouth.

DeLand, Charles. *DeLand's History of Jackson County, Michigan.* B.F. Bowen Publisher, 1903, 850. Note: this source says Isaac Quigley moved to Michigan in 1833.

1850 U.S. Census. "Isaac Quigley." ancestry.com.

Find-A-Grave. "Isaac Quigley (1763–1850)," created by Deb Hayes-Wolf. www.findagrave.com/memorial/21780474/isaac_quigley.

———. "Isaac Quigley, Jr. (1799–1849)," created by Deb Hayes-Wolf. www.findagrave.com/memorial/19323168/isaac_quigley.

———. "Samuel Quigley (1792–1860)," created by Deb Hayes-Wolf. www.findagrave.com/memorial/18658071/samuel_quigley.

Isaac Quigley (Pvt., Cpt. Quigley's Co., Col. Mitchell's Rgt., NJ Militia, American Revolution), pension no. R. 8550. *Case Files of Pension and Bounty-Land; Warrant Applications Based on Revolutionary War Service, Compiled ca. 1800–ca. 1912, Documenting the Period ca. 1775–ca. 1900.* Record Group 15; National Archives, Washington, D.C.

Museum of the American Revolution. "Remembering the Veterans of the Revolutionary War." www.amrevmuseum.org/liberty-exhibit-big-idea-7-remembering-the-veterans-of-the-revolutionary-war#:~:text=When%20soldiers%20were%20discharged%20from%20the%20Continental%20Army%2C,the%20government%20had%20no%20money%20to%20pay%20them.

U.S. General Land Office Records. "Isaac Quigley." 1776–2015.

Isaac Quigley's service is listed in the DAR and SAR registries.

According to Isaac's pension application, he was born in "the town of Nottingham, County of Burlington." Nottingham became part of Mercer County in 1838, after Isaac filed his pension.

Chapter 19

Find-A-Grave. "Andrew Swartout (1790–1859)," created by Deb Hayes-Wolfe. www.findagrave.com/memorial/19343485/andrew-swartout.

———. "James Swartout (1792–1847)," created by Deb Hayes-Wolfe. www.findagrave.com/memorial/19343380/james-swartout.

———. "Mary Cary (1797–1885)," created by Deb Hayes-Wolfe. www.findagrave.com/memorial/20777001/mary-cary.

———. "Thomas Swartout (1755–1843)," created by Deb Hayes-Wolfe. www.findagrave.com/memorial/19343371/thomas-swartout.

History. "How George Washington Used Spies to Win the American Revolution." www.history.com/news/george-washington-general-espionage-culper-spy-ring.

Jackson Citizen Patriot. "Marker-Placing Ceremony Is Held by DAR at Grave of Revolutionary Soldier." July 1, 1923.

———. "Remember Kelley's Corners?" March 20, 1956.

National Women's History Museum. "Deborah Sampson." www.womenshistory.org/education-resources/biographies/deborah-sampson.

Thomas Swartout (Pvt., Cpt. Clark's Co., Col. DunckerHoff's Rgt., NY Militia, American Revolution), pension no. S. 29490. *Case Files of Pension and Bounty-Land; Warrant Applications Based on Revolutionary War Service, Compiled ca. 1800–ca. 1912, Documenting the Period ca. 1775–ca. 1900.* Record Group 15; National Archives, Washington, D.C.

Thomas Swartout's service is "presumed" with the SAR because of his pension documents, among evidence. It is considered "NE/Not Established" with the DAR because no person has joined the DAR through his lineage.

Chapter 20

Find-A-Grave. "Elizabeth Raymond Thompson (1770–1833)," created by Twist. www.findagrave.com/memorial/87411570/elizabeth-thompson.

———. "Hiram Thompson (1800–1879)," created by Rose. www.findagrave.com/memorial/198246199/hiram-thompson.

———. "Jacob S. Thompson (unk–1861)," created Paul (Dakota) S. www.findagrave.com/memorial/14238234/jacob-thompson.

———. "John Thompson (1762–1847)," created by Deb Hayes-Wolfe. www.findagrave.com/memorial/28913971/john-thompson.

———. "John Thompson (1828–1881)," created by Memorial Searcher. www.findagrave.com/memorial/238542284/john-thompson.

History of Jackson County, Michigan. Interstate Publishing, 1881, 159.

Jonathon/John Thompson/Tompson (Pvt., Cpt. Wilson's Co., Col. Swift's Rgt., CT Line, American Revolution), pension no. W. 508. *Case Files of Pension and Bounty-Land; Warrant Applications Based on Revolutionary War Service, Compiled ca. 1800–ca. 1912, Documenting the Period ca. 1775–ca. 1900.* Record Group 15; National Archives, Washington, D.C.

Another source states Thompson died on June 1, 1847; however, an obituary for the Patriot in the May 25, 1847 local newspaper points to his death in May of that year.

John Thompson's service is listed in the DAR registry. Although no descendant has applied for membership in the SAR, that organization recognizes/accepts his service because of his pension and other documents.

The only other Thompson child to be buried in Michigan is John Thompson (1828–1881, buried Forest Hill Cemetery, Washtenaw County).

There is memorial for a "John Thompson" listed at Forest Hill Cemetery, Ann Arbor. The extensive evidence trail for his burial and grave monument in Jackson, in addition to the fact that the Ann Arbor reference does not identify a grave site, gives Jackson's specific burial site the nod.

Chapter 21

Find-A-Grave. "Daniel Thurston (1784–1854)," created by Gravedigger. www.findagrave.com/memorial/46227388/daniel_thurston.

———. "Pvt Daniel Thurston (1752–1850)," created by Deb Hayes-Wolfe. www.findagrave.com/memorial/18780256/daniel-thurston.

———. "Thomas Thurston (1786–1872)," created by Deb Hayes-Wolfe. www.findagrave.com/memorial/18780267/thomas_thurston.

History. "War of 1812." www.history.com/topics/19th-century/war-of-1812.

National Park Service. "Signal for Independence: New York Revolutionary Wars." home.nps.gov/articles/000/signal-for-independence-new-york-revolutionary-wars.htm.

Secretary of the Commonwealth. *Massachusetts Soldiers & Sailors of the American Revolution*. Vol. 15. Wright & Potter Printing Co., 1901, 714.

Thurston, Brown. *Thurston Genealogies*. 2nd ed. Brown Thurston, 1892, 59, 60, 137–39.

Daniel Thurston is listed in the SAR registry. He is considered "NE/Not Established" with the DAR because no person has joined the DAR through his lineage.

One historical account states that Thomas and his brother Daniel Jr. traveled to Buffalo in two oxcarts in 1813; however, since both Thomas and Daniel served in the war, and since only Thomas was relieved from duty due to his father's one-to-one substitution, it is not known how or why Daniel Jr. was also relieved of service so early in in the war; hence, this story focuses on its main subject—Thomas.

The only other Thurston child buried in Michigan was Daniel Thurston Jr. (1784–1854), buried in Mount Vernon Cemetery, Macomb County. See above referenced Find-A-Grave memorial for Daniel Thurston (1784–1854).

Chapter 22

Encyclopedia Britannica. "Jonathan Mayhew." www.britannica.com/biography/Jonathan-Mayhew.

Find-A-Grave. "Eri Eber Underwood (1806–1881)," created by Deb Hayes-Wolfe. www.findagrave.com/memorial/16930710/eri-eber-underwood.

———. "Jemima Fletcher Underwood (1774–1850)," created by Ancestry Pursuer. www.findagrave.com/memorial/247502936/jemima-underwood.

———. "Samuel Underwood (1767–1864)," created by Deb Hayes-Wolfe. www.findagrave.com/memorial/17199978/samuel-underwood.

Gorton, Adelos. *The Life and Times of Samuel Gorton: With a Genealogy of Samuel Gorton's Descendants to the Present Time.* George E. Furgeson Co., 1907, 425.

Lewis, Helen. *Pioneer Families of Southeastern Michigan: Especially Jackson County and New York Origins.* Kinship, 1998.

Library of Congress. "Religion and the Founding of the American Republic." www.loc.gov/exhibits/religion.

Office of the Secretary of State. *Massachusetts Soldiers and Sailors of the Revolutionary War*. Wright & Potter Printing Co., 1907, 257.

Samuel Underwood's service is "presumed" with the SAR. He is listed in the DAR registry, but future applicants must prove correct service.

Other Underwood children buried in Michigan are Lucinda J. (Underwood) Gorton (1810–1883, buried in Riverside Cemetery, Tuscola County) and Sarah (Underwood) Fielder Vaul Winney (1817–1894, buried in Oak Grove Cemetery, Washtenaw County).

Chapter 23

Find-A-Grave. "Chester C. Wall (1807–1884)," created by Frank Passic. www.findagrave.com/memorial/14918374/chester_c_wall.

———. "John Wall (1759–1849)," created by Frank Passic. www.findagrave.com/memorial/14918360/john-wall.

Jackson Citizen Patriot. "Early Days Are Recalled in Geneological [sic] Records Read on Memorial Day." June 5, 1923, 2.

John Wall (Pvt., Cpt. Mead's Co., Col. Silliman's Rgt., CT Militia, American Revolution), pension no. S. 29529. *Case Files of Pension and Bounty-Land; Warrant Applications Based on Revolutionary War Service, Compiled ca. 1800–ca. 1912, Documenting the Period ca. 1775–ca. 1900*. Record Group 15; National Archives, Washington, D.C.

New York City Revolutionary Trail. "Sugarhouse Prison." https://nycrevolutionarytrail.org/library/prison.

New York Public Library Digital Collections. "The Old Sugar House & Middle Dutch Church, Liberty St., N.Y." digitalcollections.nypl.org/items/510d47e1-2c37-a3d9-e040-e00a18064a99.

Office of the State Comptroller. *New York in the Revolution*. J.B. Lyon & Co., 1904, 131, 237.

John Wall is listed in the DAR registry. Although no descendant has applied for membership in the SAR, that organization recognizes/accepts his service.

Other Wall children buried in Michigan are Betsey (Wall) Allen (?–1865, buried in South Center Eaton Cemetery, Eaton County) and Mercy (Wall) Ostrander (1800–1869, buried in Galien Township Cemetery, Galien, Berrien County).

Chapter 24

American Battlefield Trust. "Bunker Hill." www.battlefields.org/learn/revolutionary-war/battles/bunker-hill.

Connecticut Vital Records: Lebanon, Births, Marriages & Deaths. Barbour Collection, vol. 1, 341.

Find-A-Grave. "Charles Woodworth (1785–1852)," created by Frank Passic._ findagrave.com/memorial/9258416/charles_woodworth.
———. "Swift Woodworth (1759–1838)," created by Frank Passic. www. findagrave.com/memorial/9258412/swift-woodworth.
History. "Battle of Bunker Hill." www.history.com/topics/american-revolution/ battle-of-bunker-hill._
Swift Woodworth (Pvt., Cpt. Clark's Co., Col. Strott's Rgt., CT Line, American Revolution), pension no. S. 29560. *Case Files of Pension and Bounty-Land; Warrant Applications Based on Revolutionary War Service, Compiled ca. 1800–ca. 1912, Documenting the Period ca. 1775–ca. 1900.* Record Group 15; National Archives, Washington, D.C.

Swift Woodworth is listed in the DAR registry. Although no descendant has applied for membership in the SAR, that organization recognizes/accepts his service.

An online source states that the location of Swift Woodworth's grave was based on a descendant's recollection: "a stone was put…on the site we figured was where he was buried." For more information on the source, see the previously referenced Find-A-Grave citation. The authors concur that Woodworth is indeed buried in West Concord Cemetery for the reasons stated in the text.

Other sources list Woodworth's birthplace as "Windham," Connecticut. There is no inconsistency since his pension application lists his place of birth as "Town of Lebanon, County of Windham." Also, another source lists his date of death as May 5, 1838. In his pension records, however, Swift's son consistently writes to the federal government seeking arrears of his father's pension up to March 5, 1838. It is never stated as the date of death, but there is no reference in the government documents of a death date of May 5, 1838. Thus, assuming the pension is paid up to the death of the pensioner, the authors have deduced that the date of death is March 5. If Swift had died on May 5, 1838, his son likely would have sought the additional three months of back pension as well, but he did not. March 5 is also listed on the headstone application.

Chapter 25

Find-A-Grave. "B. Buirne (1732–1811)," created by Jeannieology.
———. "Henry Durand (1787–1863)," created by Frank Passic. www.findagrave.com/memorial/8241592/henry-lovewell.
———. "John Durand (1770–1852)," created by Deb Hayes-Wolfe. www. findagrave.com/memorial/16452052/john-durand.
———. "Samuel Graham, Sr. (1762–1840)," created by Sandra Rosenbrook Graham. [please add web address here]
———. "William Champe (1755–1834)," created by Jeannieology.
Portrait and Biographical Album of Jackson County, Michigan, Containing Full Page Portraits and Biographical Sketches, Portraits & Biographies of All the Governors of the

State and of the Presidents of the United States. Chapman Brothers, 1890, 529, 582; refers to William Lovewell migrating to Jackson with son Henry and that he was a Patriot.

B. Buirne's service is considered "NE/Not Established" with the DAR because no person has joined the DAR through his lineage. He is not listed in the SAR registry.

John Durand's service is considered "NE/Not Established" with the DAR because no person has joined the DAR through his lineage. He is not listed in the registry.

Samuel Graham is not listed in the DAR or SAR registries.

William Champe is not listed in the DAR or SAR registries.

William (father of Henry Durand) Lovewell is not listed in the DAR or SAR registries.

Chapter 26

Jackson Citizen Patriot. "Bloodstained Drum Was Found in Attic of Home Where Descendant of Drummer Boy Lived; Is Now in the Possession of A.T. Curtis." February 2, 1934.

Larrison, Brad. "Revolution Museum Teaches How Fife and Drums Were Tools of War." WHYY, PBS, August 19, 2017. whyy.org/articles/revolution-museum-teaches-how-fife-and-drums-were-tools-of-war.

Chapter 27

Encyclopedia Britannica. "King George II." www.britannica.com/biography/George-II-king-of-Great-Britain.

Detroit Historical Society. "French Detroit." detroithistorical.org/learn/timeline-detroit/french-detroit-1700-1760.

Gerych, Scott, chairman of the Michigan Military Heritage Museum. Interview, June 26, 2024.

The Historical Marker Database. "Fort Pontchartrain." www.hmdb.org/m.asp?m=21853.

Miscellaneous Technical Articles. "British Cannon Design 1600–1800." www.arc.id.au/Cannon.html.

ABOUT THE AUTHORS

David Van Hoof grew up in Jackson, Michigan, and is a graduate of Lumen Christi High School. Upon receiving his bachelor of arts from the University of Michigan and juris doctorate from Detroit College of Law, he enlisted in the United States Marine Corps, retiring as a major after twenty-two years of service. During his military career, he earned additional graduate degrees from the University of Oklahoma and Arizona State University in public administration, international history, public history and World War II studies. He currently resides in Douglas, Michigan, with his wife, Alissa, and is actively involved in the National Society Sons of the American Revolution.

Linda Hass is a Jackson, Michigan–based author/researcher/presenter who specializes in local history. Linda has a master's degree in journalism (sub-specialty in history) from Michigan State University. She has authored three previous books and researched and successfully applied for four state historical markers and three national designations from the National Park Service. She serves as an officer of the Jackson County, Michigan Historical Society and was named "Jackson Historian" by the Jackson City Council in 2021. When she is not giving tours, exploring cemeteries or traveling to archives and museums, Linda and her husband, Ed, enjoy long walks in the country and frying a batch of freshly caught fish.